Rob Wagner's Script

AUGUST 1, 1942

Ye Ed

(See Page 5)

The Best of
Rob Wagner's Script

edited by
ANTHONY SLIDE

The Scarecrow Press, Inc.
Metuchen, N.J., & London
1985

Library of Congress Cataloging in Publication Data
Main entry under title:

The Best of Rob Wagner's Script.

   Includes index.
   1. Moving-pictures--Reviews. 2. Theater--Reviews.
3. American fiction--20th century. 4. American essays--
20th century. I. Wagner, Rob, 1872-1942. II. Slide,
Anthony. III. Script (Beverly Hills, Calif.)
PN1995.B375 1985   791.43'0973   85-2315
ISBN 0-8108-1810-8

Copyright © 1985 by Anthony Slide

Manufactured in the United States of America

CONTENTS

Introduction, by Anthony Slide	v
Will Rogers--Fool, by Rob Wagner	1
A Tribute from a Great Director to a "Great Actor," by Ernst Lubitsch	6
The New Ballerina, by Agnes George de Mille	6
What's Wrong with Musical Pictures?, by Sigmund Romberg	9
A Problem in Chivalry, by Tom Mix	14
Technocracy: The New Hope, by Upton Sinclair	16
Mizner the Magnificent, by Jim Tully	20
Gertrude Stein and Mae West, by Richard Sheridan Ames	24
Charlie Chaplin's First Story	27
Frank Capra, by Jim Tully	30
Los Angeles--A Pain in the Neck to New York, by Don Herold	33
Nocturne, by Charlie Chaplin	41
So He Died Laughing, by William Saroyan	41
Or Leave a Kiss Within the Cup, by William Saroyan	44
Will Rogers, by Rob Wagner	46
Boy O Boy O Boy, O Boy, by William Saroyan	51
How to Be a Writer, by William Saroyan	56
Crazy Hollywood, by William Saroyan	58
The Unknown Soldier Speaks, by Eddie Cantor	63
Fascismo Americano, by Philip Dunne	64
The End of the World, by William Saroyan	67
Nigger: Saying Good-By, by Dore Schary	73
Outline of Eccentricity, by Irving Wallace	76
Rhythm, by Charles Chaplin	80
Experiment in the Dark, by Charles Chaplin	82
Shanghai, Not Without Gestures, by Louis L'Amour	87
Little Orson Annie, by Gene Lockhart	92
Show Me the Way to Go Home, by Louis L'Amour	93
To Make a Long Story Much Shorter, by Ray Bradbury	98

The Mikado--1942, by Gene Lockhart 101
Epilogue by an Old Pupil, by José Rodriguez 105
Give Us More Bombs over Berlin, by Charles Chaplin 108
I Like to Remember, by Eddie Cantor 111
Comics and the War, by Eddie Cantor 113
Example, by Jessamyn West 116
Through a Glass Darkly, by Jessamyn West 116
A Salute to Russia, by Charlie Chaplin 117
The Common Man, by Ben Hecht 117
Those Griffith Girls, by Herb Sterne 130
The Fool, by Charlie Chaplin 134
D. W. G. : A Poet Sings in Celluloid, by Herb Sterne 137
Iris Barry: The Attila of Films, by Herb Sterne 140
Skeleton, by Ray Bradbury 144
Alla Be Praised, by Herb Sterne 148
Joan Crawford: Erstwhile Dancing Daughter, by Herb Sterne 152
Electric Shadows, by James Wong Howe 156
Carlton Moss: Our Cover Boy, by Dalton Trumbo 161
The Outlaw Rides Again, by Louis L'Amour 165
Screen, by Lillian Gish 168

Index to Contributors 173

INTRODUCTION

Who was Rob Wagner and what was his Script? In an age of such press barons as Rupert Murdoch and such glossy, intellectually slim periodicals as People and US, in an era in which a highly personal general magazine is unthinkable, Rob Wagner's Script must appear almost antediluvian. Rob Wagner's Script was not particularly solid, in the manner of Atlantic Monthly or even Esquire, and its articles were usually no more than two pages in length, but it was a remarkable, though certainly small, journal with a fiercely loyal readership, published in Beverly Hills, and intended, basically, for the more intelligent citizens of that community. Indeed, for the first seven months of its life, the magazine was titled Rob Wagner's Beverly Hills Script. It combined new fiction with regular columns and humor, rather in the manner of The New Yorker, and might well be considered the West Coast equivalent of that venerable New York journal. Script's cartoons were never as funny as those in The New Yorker, and it would often utilize the same drawing, year after year, with different captions. Nor were Script's profiles or short stories as lengthy as those in The New Yorker, but they were certainly as well written, and both journals shared one or two of the same contributors, particularly Don Herold and Ted Cook.

First published February 16, 1929, as Rob Wagner's Beverly Hills Script, the magazine dropped the "Beverly Hills" on August 17 of that year. Script appeared weekly until 1939, when it became a fortnightly publication. It remained under the editorial control of Rob Wagner and his family until March 1, 1947, when it was sold, changed its name to simply Script, and appeared on a monthly basis under the editorship of James P. Felton until March 1949. Rob Wagner, "Ye Ed," as he always referred to himself, died on July 20, 1942, and the editorship was assumed by his wife, Florence, who had been involved with the magazine since its inception, and, for a

v

while, by Wagner's son, Leicester, a San Francisco-based newspaperman. (While Rob and Florence Wagner were on a round-the-world tour in the late thirties, the magazine was edited by Tom Moriarty.)

Rob Wagner was, by all accounts, a unique character. Born in Detroit on August 2, 1872, he had been a student at the University of Michigan and studied art in Paris before becoming an artist with the Detroit Free Press. He came to Los Angeles in the early years of this century and in 1914 joined the faculty of the Manual Arts High School, where he taught athletics and art to such pupils as Frank Capra, General James Doolittle, Lawrence Tibbett, and José Rodriguez, who became a frequent contributor to Script (and whose tribute to Wagner is included in this anthology). In 1915, Wagner also added Greek to the subjects which he taught; according to the Los Angeles Times, "Someone asked him if he could teach it and he said he would look Greece up on the map and begin studying so he could and did."

Wagner's interest in motion pictures dates back to 1909, when he first met Hobart Bosworth, then with the Selig Polyscope Company, and began to write a series of articles on the fledgling industry for The Saturday Evening Post, Collier's and other periodicals. His contributions as a filmmaker are not particularly impressive. Wagner directed only one feature, a 1924 Walter Hiers comedy vehicle titled Fair Week, and provided screenplays for a number of minor features from 1921 to 1928, starring the likes of cowboy star Lefty Flynn, as well as a couple of Charles Ray features, R. S. V. P. (1921) and Smudge (1924). Wagner's best known work in the film industry is the direction of the 1924 Will Rogers' parody of The Covered Wagon, titled Two Wagons--Both Covered. It is possible that Wagner assisted in the production of a number of other Will Rogers' Hal Roach/Pathe shorts, and certainly he and Rogers remained firm friends until the latter's death in 1935. Rob Wagner also published an anecdotal volume on the film community titled Film Folk (The Century Company, 1918), as well as two pamphlets, Picture Values from an Artist's Viewpoint (Palmer Photoplay Corporation, 1920) and Two Decades: The Story of a Man of God--Hollywood's Own Padre (the Reverend Neal Dodd), co-authored with Rupert Hughes (Young & McCallister, 1936).

Rob Wagner's close ties to the motion picture community are very apparent in the pages of Script. Many of the articles deal in one way or another with the entertainment industry, and the journal boasts such contributors as Charles Chaplin, Ernst Lubitsch, Alan Mowbray, Noel Madison, and other film personalities. Wagner was also quick to realize that it would be a good idea for his advertisers to be aware of just how many stars, directors, producers, and writers had paid subscriptions to Script, and so at least once a year, he would publish a listing of those to whom Script was sent regularly. Wagner never let his readers forget that they were part of his family, that Script was basically a small, intimate journal for those select few who appreciated the finer things of life, particularly life in Beverly Hills.

On Script's eighth anniversary (February 13, 1937) "Ye Ed" wrote,

> Script is not just Rob Wagner; it is a spiritual entity composed of all these writers and artists, plus the most extraordinarily interested and enthusiastic lot of readers in the country. "I'd rather write for Script than for any of the big-pay magazines." "Rob, don't let Script go national; let's keep it as it is." We hear these two expressions every day, and they intrinsically carry the thought that both contributors and readers consider Script their magazine.

What is remarkable about Script is that for most of its life it paid almost none of its contributors. One can, perhaps, understand, why young and hopeful writers, such as William Saroyan (whose earliest work appeared in Script), Louis L'Amour or Ray Bradbury, were happy to adopt such an outlet. But it can only be thanks to the good feeling generated by Rob Wagner that Jim Tully or Don Herold or Upton Sinclair were willing, unpaid contributors.

Among the regular writers for Script were screenwriter Marion Fairfax, art director Harry Oliver, Judge Leon R. Yankwich, John Hanlon, Paul Gerard Smith, A. Beverly Coote, Alfred Count, and Edward Bernds. Alan Mowbray contributed two one-act plays to Script (in November and December of 1936) and from 1943 onwards wrote the "Hollywood V-Hive" column. Grace La Rue's autobiography, "My Vaudeville Years," was published from September-October 1937. Among the regular columns were "High Spots" by Cornelius Vanderbilt, Jr., "London Notes" by Richard Willis (taken over in 1937 by actor Noel Madison, and in April 1941 by Clarence Winchester), "Book Stuff" by Mrs. Jack Vallely, "Radiophonics" by Dale Armstrong (a column of radio criticism which began in April 1939), "Art Stuff" by Buckley MacGurrin, "Paris Notes" by Carol Weld, "The San Francisco Scene" by Tom Moriarty, "Chicago Notes" by Donald Plant, "Smithereens" by Paul Gerard Smith, "Nature Stuff" by Vance Hoyt, and "Weisscrax" by David Weissman.

Theatre and film reviews were initially handled by Rob and Florence Wagner, then by Richard Sheridan Ames, and eventually by Herb Sterne (who also wrote on Los Angeles nightlife under the pseudonym of "Dan Rich"). New York theatre reviews were contributed by various writers, notably DeWitt Bodeen, Frank Vreeland and Russell Rhoades. After the journal passed from Florence Wagner's control, Kenneth Macgowan became film critic for a while.*

Rob Wagner was an old-fashioned liberal. From the safety and security of Beverly Hills, he could easily concern himself with the plight of the poor and downtrodden, and Wagner's liberal stance led to his publishing pieces by Upton Sinclair, Ben Hecht and even a salute to Russia by Charles Chaplin. (Of course, Wagner's liberal viewpoint did not prevent his applauding Douglas Fairbanks' idea of building a wall around Beverly Hills to keep out riffraff from Los Angeles!)

Gathered together for this anthology are what I consider the best pieces--fiction and nonfiction--that appeared in Rob Wagner's Script. I have not included any of the regular columns, although I have included essays by three columnists: Richard Sheridan Ames, José Rodriguez and Herb Sterne. I have limited Rob Wagner's contributions to two masterful studies of Will Rogers, one written when Rogers was at the height of his popularity and one written shortly after the humorist's death. As far as I can ascertain none of the "celebrity" pieces were ghost-written.

Anthony Slide

---

*Many of the film and theatre reviews from Rob Wagner's Script are reprinted in the Selected Film Criticism and Selected Theatre Criticism series, both published by Scarecrow Press.

WILL ROGERS--FOOL

by Rob Wagner

Uneasy Lies the Head

Several years ago, a King* and a Fool were trainmates coming to California. The King, a kindly, elderly man beloved of his family, friends and even his subjects, had just experienced a painful ordeal at Court, and though he had been acquitted of unkingly conduct, he was distressed in mind and body. As the train rolled down through the familiar orange groves of Riverside County, and more familiar oil wells of Santa Fe Springs, he smiled wistfully. He was returning home, where at least his own people would understand.

The Fool was also coming home after a long stay in the East, where he had been Fooling in a Follies Show to the hilarious joy of both Cabbages and Kings.

Kings Should Wear Their Crowns

As the train pulled into the station, the King, worn and haggard, appeared upon the platform, and as he gazed out over the huge throng gathered there, a light of happy relief came into his graying eyes. This was indeed a welcome! Several thousand of his beloved home-folk here to pay him friendly tribute! Not only the peasantry; his Ministers of State, high city officials, great bankers and brother Kings of Industry awaited his debarkation. Stepping from the train, the King was instantly surrounded by high-hatted official welcomers who formed an Imperial Guard as they led him through the packed lines toward the Royal Coach. Wistfully hungry for sympathy, the King looked into the faces of his subjects for signs of kindly sympathy, but strangely enough, they seemed not to

*The King in this essay is presumably Douglas Fairbanks, Sr.

know him. Perhaps it was awed embarrassment. The King smiled bravely as he passed through the station into the street beyond.

Two Homecomings

Emerging upon the sidewalk, the King's face quickly broke into a happy smile as a deafening cheer arose, and he beheld a vast crowd waving countless flags. But just as suddenly his face went chalky white again. Those vivacious symbols were not for him! "Welcome to the new Mayor of Beverly Hills!" "Bill Rogers, the One and Only!" they read. Nor the cheers. They were for a grinning, gum-chewing man following the Royal entourage down those lines of yelling and confetti-throwing villagers. The demonstration was for the Fool!

Few there were in all that mad assemblage who noted the little drama being enacted under their excited noses. Those who did, observed the King inconspicuously hurried to his waiting coach, while the Fool was borne to a flower-embowered chariot, which, followed by an immense procession of gaily decorated automobiles, started on a triumphant journey across the great metropolis towards the Fool's hometown, acclaimed en route by thousands and thousands of happy bystanders who shouted friendly greetings. The King was escorted to the same beautiful destination, but his carriage attracted no more attention than the humblest Ford in the immensity of a city's traffic.

Shakespeare Knew the Answer

Nor was that the end of the living drama. Later in the day, an immense crowd of happy villagers gathered in the Park and, to the blare of bands, waving of flags and tumultuous cheering, elevated the Fool to the highest honor they could bestow. They made him Honorary Mayor of their Beloved City.

In contrast to this scene of carnival, the King, high up in his castle on the hill, paced its lonesome corridors, and though he could not see the ceremonies, he no doubt heard the cheering. In any event, he had seen and heard enough to give him pause and no doubt cause him to ponder on the immemorial question of why the world prefers Fools to Kings.

Will Rogers--Fool

A Holy Priesthood

In fact that is why we have painted this little picture. We, too, have pondered the question of why the world sometimes tolerates its Kings, but loves its Fools. We think the reason is because in a World of Pain we love the person who can make us laugh, and in laughing, forget pain. Thus we honor Magnificent Fools--Mark Twain, George Ade, Charlie Chaplin, Montague Glass, Franklin P. Adams, Ted Cook, Bugs Baer, O. O. McIntyre, Harold Lloyd, George Herriman, and a host of others who wave the Cap and Bells. While a mad Emperor was leading his people to ruin, Germany forbade its actors, especially comedians, going to the front. They were needed to keep the nation sane.

The Wisdom of Fools

Why, we may ask again, did Shakespeare put his wisest sayings into the mouths of his Fools? Because that great dramatist knew that only great philosophers could be great Fools. Not that all philosophers are Fools--some of them are solemn asses, but every great Fool is a philosopher. He must see life clearly, unimpressed by sham and show. Fools are the supreme critics of our times, noting our foibles, weaknesses and idiosyncrasies and making us take their critiques by serving them in capsules of humor so that we do not taste the bitterness or sting. It is only the superficial judge who regards the Fool as merely an entertainer. If the Fool has become an Institution, one may be sure there lurks within him the soul of a great philosopher.

We Honor a Great Fool

No, the Fool we are banqueting tonight is anything but a fool. He is, in fact, one of the greatest Philosophers America has produced. Lurking back of that whimsical exterior is the Superior Man who must, indeed, even though subconsciously, feel his superiority over little fools. Else how can he puncture the solemn sham of the world's Kings? We have heard cowboys claim that they could twirl a rope as well as Will, but that Will got the "breaks." But Ziegfeld did not pay Will three thousand dollars a week for twirling a rope. Nor did he pay him that huge sum for merely smart-cracking. It was the content of those smart cracks that lifted the great entertainer so far above his fellows. For Will's "gags," as he calls them, are critiques, epigrammatic editorials, and satirical comments on our national institutions and personal idiosyncrasies. The slow and ponderous workings of the usual philosophic mind are not Will's; his wit works in brilliant flashes, with a psychic understanding almost feminine. The Follies gags that made him famous were inspired by reading late evening papers five minutes before going on to do his act. Next morning his classic wheezes appeared in thousands of papers throughout the country. "If I happened to hit on religion, Ziegfeld would stand in the wings and wring his hands," he told us one day, "but I always worked the gag around so that in the end I gave the fellow I was kidding the best of it." It is this essential fairness and natural kindness of heart that has permitted the King of Fools to kid our Kings, and not incur the displeasure of his victims. Only a Fool secure in his exalted position would dare impersonate a President of the United States.

A Fan's Reward

Will's gentler moments are quite as fine as his public gags. He was reading his fan mail in his dressing room. One letter was from a chap in Connecticut. "He says he's been to see all my pictures," Will mumbled as he read along. "And I guess he has, for he's named over several that I'd clean forgot about.... He says he has to walk seven miles to town to the movie theatre.... And," Will grinned, "--and he wants m' photygraf."

"You'll send it to him, won't you?" we asked.

Will took another chew on his gum and replied: "Well I think I oughta send him a horse."

A Charming Refusal

On another occasion we were working on Two Wagons-- Both Covered* at his house when a man called from the Ford agency in Los Angeles to say that Mr. Ford had wired asking him to have Will go down and select a Lincoln car which the great automobile builder wished to present to his friend.

---

*A two-reel Hal Roach/Pathe short released on January 6, 1924.

Will was obviously embarrassed, and after hemming and hawing, he sent the fellow away with the assurance that he would reply to Mr. Ford directly. Later in the evening he prepared a telegram for us to take to the office. It read:

"Thanks, Henry. But if it's all the same to you, I'll take eleven Fords and a tractor. I've always wanted to know how it feels to get up in the morning and go out and just choose a car. Will Rogers."

A Fool Who Is a King Maker

In the field of politics Will Rogers has become a terrific force in American life. So deep is his understanding of men and events and so incisive his wit that even the greatest statesmen seek his favor. A boost from Will is worth millions of votes; his kidding is likely to mean political oblivion. Furthermore, just as Cervantes laughed Chivalry out of Europe, so Will Rogers can crystalize or destroy a political issue with his editorial "gags." Wise philosopher that he is, he never takes strong party sides. Nobody knows how he votes, and by thus taking a philosophic station on the side-lines he can criticise and laugh at the entire show. That he should ever run for or accept political office is unthinkable, for nobody knows better than he that it would end him as the great political commentator. Furthermore, he is doubtless aware that we laugh at Fools but we vote for Bryans. Lincoln's Fooling was discovered only after he was elected.

To Will--Philosopher, Citizen, Wit!

Thus do we understand the manner of man we are entertaining tonight, not as a mere comedian who makes us laugh, but as one of the greatest and kindliest philosophers that ever illumined the minds of men.

--Vol. 1, No. 17 (June 8, 1929), pages 1-3.

A TRIBUTE FROM A GREAT DIRECTOR
TO A "GREAT ACTOR"

by Ernst Lubitsch

Dear Bob:

     Permit me to contribute a paragraph to your page of motion picture criticism. Last night I went to the Carthay Circle Theatre to see Will Rogers in his first talking picture, They Had to See Paris. Marvelous! I was astonished at Will Rogers' work. To call him a comedian is unjust to his art--the word is too small. He is one of the greatest HUMORISTS I have ever seen, but he is also a great ACTOR! His characterization was not of one small-town garage owner in Oklahoma, but of every small-town garage owner in America. This [Frank] Borzage picture was one of the few I have seen that I was sorry to have end.

                  Enthusiastically yours,
                                  Ernst Lubitsch.

                  --Vol. 2, No. 11 (October 26, 1929), page 14.

THE NEW BALLERINA

by Agnes George de Mille

The day of the great solo dancers is unquestionably on the wane. Karsavina, Anna Pavlowa and Argentina are the last of that illustrious procession of charming women who have used the dance to exploit their own personalities, their seductiveness, beauty, technique or emotional force. When these are gone the last spangled skirt will have swirled into history to join the tradition of Comargo, Taglioni and Genée, utterly lovely, magical women whose presence epitomized the romance

The New Ballerina 7

and beauty of their epoch, whose art was the flowering of whole social systems. Their satin feet have marched ahead of armies. Poets have learned from their gauzes, cities waited for their smile. Their tambourines have set the tune of music.

When Pavlowa takes the scene the Russian Empire rises again, the Czar's court, the men who have loved her, the composers who have worked for her, the gallantry of all the audiences of the cities of Europe. She treads the stage in glamour. Her beauty is the culmination of great traditions. Part of the work which earns her applause was done by women dead two hundred years. And whether styles crumble or stand or hordes of dancers share her stage or leave it, the presence of "great theatre" exists where she is, regardless of her ballets, her assistants or her décor. Her ballets are forgotten as soon as she dances them. The lift of her body and her smile are immortal.

In place of the heroic courtesan of the last five hundred years the star dancer is today little more than a severe, capable teamworker. Two factors have combined to bring about this change: the lack of subsidized orgnizations to foster and display the art of such women, and a reconception of the function of the dance itself. Anna Pavlowa developed her technique in a school under the supervision of the Czar. All her girlhood was passed in gracious contact with the painters, musicians, writers and rulers of her country. When she was graduated at seventeen she fell heir with the other students in her class to a subsidized theater devoted entirely to ballet dancing, a working organization of artistic experts, a large repertoire of roles, and an audience trained since birth in the highly technicalized vocabulary of her art. She had only to keep her mind on dancing better than any other living person. No other consideration bothered her.

The concert dancers must now find unaided a technical education, a mature expression of form, a theatre in which to display their work, a program of presentation for their work, and an audience that will not come to them ignorant of all the fine points of the art of dancing. Girls wait on tables in order to continue with their career. They starve themselves. They waste themselves in drudgery that can help them in no way professionally. Few are magnetic enough or lucky enough to win through alone. They band together, of necessity, under a leader who serves as their teacher, discard the traditional idea of soloist and corps de ballet and work as a group expressing group ideas. The leaders are themselves stars in the true sense of the word, but they differ from their predecessors in this--they are quite as interested in the group and the group's dances as they are in their own personal triumph.

A change in the conception of dancing itself would follow obviously as a result of the influence of economic pressure on the dancers. Certainly, also, the revolution in artistic thought which has swept Europe, due in its turn to political and economic shake-ups, has made itself felt in all the schools and concert groups. In every branch of art, the emphasis has been turned from the romantic problem of the individual in relation to beauty to that of the individual in relation to the community and the problems of communal living. Dances deal now almost exclusively with folk material, rituals, legends, parables, moralities, race studies. In England folk dance societies have been formed which include an appreciable percentage of the middle class population. In Germany the great schools of dancing devote their entire energy to the study of group movement. The Duncan dancers of Moscow are subsidized by the state and boast no outstanding soloists except Irma, who is more of a teacher than anything else. Their finest work is unquestionably their interpretation of the Soviet labor songs.

In Harlem the Negroes are dancing the melancholy of a subject people and the thwarting of primitive needs. The whites in the Metropolitan theatres are borrowing the Negroes' form to express their own depression and hungers. The concert dancers likewise concern themselves with the frenzy of American civilization, and in psychological studies built on the Blues pattern of stylized gesture and rhythm, give graphic analyses of the effect of the civilization on the individual. It is interesting to note that it was the American Isadora who first brought back religion to the stage, and the American St. Denis who first reproduced thereon specific rituals.

One has only to compare the titles of dances in the old order with new ones to comprehend the amazing difference. For instance, "The Spirit of Champagne," "Coppelia, or The Girl with the Enamel Eyes" (Genée), "The Death of the Swan," "The Dragonfly," "The Coquetteries of Columbine" (Pavlowa), "The Fire Bird," "Le Spectre de la Rose," "Carneval" (Karsavina), as against "Heretic," "Strike," "Adolescence," "Visions of the Apocalypse" (Martha Graham), "The Life of the Bee" (Doris Humphreys), "Revolt," "Three

The New Ballerina 9

Mad Figures," "The Angel of the Last Judgment" (Kreutzberg), "The Prodigal Son," "The Rites of Spring" (Diagheleff Ballet).

On the stages of the world not less than on the levees or the plains the dancers are performing the rituals of mating, harvesting, appeasing the gods, keeping or breaking the race rules. Folk drama has left the public square and common and is in our theatre. The people are again taken into the dance. It has come back to its ancient traditional place of a communal rite.

What are our professional folkdancers like? Lean-limbed and serious-minded, scorning femininity of manner or dress, they wear symbolic shifts, run up and down symbolic platforms and steps, submerge their personalities almost completely in the effort to project an idea. The enormous priced stars of the Diagheleff Ballet are today as alike as a row of beanpoles. Possessed of great personal beauty, fabulous technique, and remarkable feeling for style, they are as difficult to distinguish one from another as the members of a football team in action. Alas, they cannot perform the old beloved dances. Sokolowa and Karsavina still dominate their scene like peacocks among wood pheasants. But watch the younger women in the new ballets. Theirs is the beauty of precision, coordination, clarity and unity of understanding.

The tambourines have ceased to tinkle. The ruffled skirts are dropped in the wings. The stage is stormed by shafts of light, naked bodies, and companies and companies of unknown dancers working in common spontaneous purpose.

--Vol. 3, No. 74 (July 12, 1930), pages 16-17.

WHAT'S WRONG WITH MUSICAL PICTURES?

by Sigmund Romberg

Note by Ed: Though he has modestly omitted his own name from this article, Mr. Romberg is one of America's most famous musical composers. His best known works are <u>Blossom Time</u>, <u>The Student Prince</u>, <u>The Desert Song</u>, and <u>New Moon</u>. Having just finished <u>Viennese Nights</u>, in collaboration with Oscar Hammerstein 2nd, Mr. Romberg is now engaged upon the score of <u>Children of Dreams</u>, his second operetta written especially for the screen.

Music accompanies us from the cradle to the grave--from "Rock-a-bye, Baby," to Chopin's "Funeral March." We sing, march and dance to music. There is music in our schools, churches and play places. White men, brown men, yellow men, and black men--all are attuned to music. Music is the universal language. Music is part and parcel of life. Yes, and after death, the heavenly choir!

What, then, is wrong with our musical pictures? Why is it that music and dancing are failing on the screen? It can't be music per se; it must be the way it is being played. Perhaps a study of the stage will give the answer, for there, too, music has faced difficult problems which have been solved only by years of experimentation.

Out of fifty productions a year in New York, only ten are musicals. The reason is twofold--the cost and the scarcity of musician-composers.

An ordinary drama requires a cast of from six to perhaps sixteen characters; two or, at most, three sets; weekly expenses of from fifteen hundred to five thousand dollars, and a road try-out of two or three weeks. In case of failure, the loss may not be more than fifteen or twenty thousand dollars.

A musical show, on the other hand, requires a huge cast, a large singing and dancing ensemble, a big orchestra, innumerable sets, and a horde of electricians and stage hands. A single musical number in an operetta will often cost more than a whole dramatic production.

By the time a musical show has reached the try-out period on the road, the producer is in perhaps sixty or seventy thousand dollars. And so, of course, he must go on investing more and more in order to save his initial investment.

What's Wrong with Musical Pictures? 11

The possible results, of course, justify the gamble, for the musical show can demand a much higher toppprice than ordinary drama. If successful, it will play to the extraordinary grosses of from thirty to fifty thousand dollars a week. For every such production, however, there will be five which will just get by or fail entirely.

We now come to the sudden invention of the audible film. Realizing that music was now possible in moving pictures, the producers set forth in a mad scramble to import every song writer and dance impresario in New York to come to Hollywood and make musical whoopee for the masses. Untrained in the technique of musical construction, the executives thought all they had to do was assemble a lot of musical and dancing numbers and then let nature and the cutting room take their course. The result was a jumble of this and that with no definite score, complete absence of story, and the inclusion of songs that had nothing to do with anything, but which the producers hoped to force into popularity.

The producers next began to gather in all the musical shows and operettas that had ever seen the boards, failures as well as successes. Better grab everything in sight lest the other fellow get it. But here again, they depended upon their own staffs. They bought the productions, but not the men who had produced them. The result was added slaughter of fine material.

With an entirely new medium and no standard pattern, no new form having been invented, tried and found satisfactory, every studio had to create itw own method--and bedlam reigned.

Songs, the primitive form of a musical score, were the first elements employed. Songs, songs, songs! At every opportunity a song. Stars with no voices were made to sing. Songs were written overnight by the new army of song writers. Songs of moons, songs of coons; songs of loves and songs of doves; flowers, bowers, blues and booze. No picture, howsoever dramatic, but must be punctuated with songs.

Even the successful operettas purchased in hysteria had to be broken down and operated upon to conform with the new movie technique. The new songs from the song hands on heavy salary must be included. For you must remember that one song hit, howsoever foreign to the artistic whole, might--through radio and other rights--pay for the cost of production.

Then, again, the operetta must be changed to satisfy the looks of the star or the mood of the director, or to "give the gravy" to this person or that. The score which made that operetta popular in London, New York, Paris, Berlin and Australia--which was the essential backbone of a production--was changed overnight by song writers with new songs.

Did the movie producers realize the difference between a score and a song? Did any of them stop to think that a score is a unit of melodies written after careful consideration, by graduation, to bring an audience into a certain mood, or frame of mind, as the book may require? Nobody knew, or cared, that in a score, a composer, from the opening note to the closing bar, through skillful manipulation of different tempos, with different instrumentations, through different songs, plays for two and a half hours with an audience and sells them something so satisfactory that, by the end of the evening, they go out whistling his numbers and recommending the show to their friends.

Songs, of course, are also part of a score. But not even a successful song will make a bad score good; while, in a cleverly manipulated score, one or two songs written, of course, by the same composer who writes his own score, will stick out and satisfy the demand. Compare a bungalow with a ten-story building, and you will have the same ratio as a song with a score.

But time was pressing and songs replaced the score in the hurry to produce. So bedlam broke out again, not noticed at first, on account of the rush and the newness of the whole thing. There was a rush to release, popular openings with lights and whatnot--and then the result? Apathy from the movie audiences, who, of course, didn't know and didn't care under what circumstances these musical pieces were gotten up. At first the novelty of music surmounted the handicap. But the sameness and monotony of singing and dancing in the wrong place, at the wrong time, and in the wrong way, got past the mark of endurance, and people simply refused to have anything to do with musicals.

The song writers, some of them masters in their individual art, were the first to realize that something was

What's Wrong with Musical Pictures?

missing, but unfortunately, nobody else did--or even wanted to listen to them. The staggering figure of two hundred or three hundred new songs per month also became ridiculous and utterly beyond the receptivity of the picture audiences. The Broadway producer of musical shows, who took his show on the road before bringing it to New York, could change music if his author or composer were wrong. He could change his cast and keep fixing up and changing until the best results were obtained, bringing a finished production into New York.

Not so with the movie producers. Once something was recorded and photographed, it had to stay. The clamor for pictures was so great and the demand for supply so vehement that everything had to be released at once.

The break came. It came gradually until every studio realized that the procedure was absolutely wrong, and that in order to produce a successful musical picture, different technique and different knowledge must be employed. The studios learned, too, that every emotion in the picture requires thought and that only persons with experience, who have made music a life study, are the right ones to undertake the making of musical pictures.

A complete change of policy is the result. From now on, instead of producing forty musicals a year, each studio will make three or four. Instead of having six or seven writers, lyricists, and song writers prepare something for the same purpose, men like Jerome Kern, Oscar Straus, Harry Tierney, Rudolph Friml, and Richard Rodgers will compose original scores for pictures, for which the original books will be made by such outstanding artists as Oscar Hammerstein 2nd, Otto Harbach, Ernest Vajda, Herbert Fields, and Anne Caldwell.

Will the movie audiences like this new type of work? Time alone will tell. But, at least, it will be tried by the most successful writers, and if this set of authors can't make it go, nothing will.

--Vol. 3, No. 77 (August 2, 1930), pages 6-7.

A PROBLEM IN CHIVALRY

by Tom Mix

How we going to save 'em when the rip tide gets 'em? Where we going to grab 'em--and yet be gentlemen!

    That's what some of us fellers who do a little summer swimming 'round the beaches would like to know. We'd be obliged if Beatrice Fairfax, Emily Post, George Bernard Shaw, [H. L.] Mencken, or some of these birds who seem to known and write about almost anything, would send a few kindly and instructing lines on this subject and send 'em pronto.

    Today, on any Atlantic or Pacific beach--excepting perhaps, Old Orchard or Asbury Park--our problem confronts us--a comely, up-to-the-minute young miss, wearing one of these new streamline, backless, almost frontless, part-time strapless, 1932 bathing suits. It stands to reason that now and then the pinkish young party of the first part is a-going to get a coupla splashes too far out, and somebody's got to bring her in. How?

    Miss Fairfax and Miss Post would probably advise: "Call the life guard."

    Imagine the problem of the suntanned, clean-minded young life guard who is battling a tough tide-rip with the banker's beautiful daughter in tow. She's clad--or unclad--in one of these low-geared free-wheelers, and the rescuer realizes a little more rip either way will settle the question. If she hasn't even the straps--what then?

    The U.S. Life Guard Rules, Page three, paragraph three, put it down that struggling misses are to be towed in by the back of the bathing suit. Okay, for Old Orchard and Asbury Park and Long Beach, California, where they still play croquet, give rook parties and wear skirts on their bathing suits. But what are we going to do on the other beaches where the girls favor wide open spaces in bathing suit construction?

A Problem in Chivalry 15

My experience is that girls don't want to be towed in with that tender care given to a case that's been tossed over by an escaping rumrunner--the girls want to struggle--it's more romantic--they insist upon one of those powerful aquatic combats pictured in the movies. They demand plenty of footage.

A lot of beach rescues are like a proposition in Euclid: given--a pretty girl, a new and attractive bathing suit, a lot of water, a crowded beach, good-looking young men standing around, a few handy life guards and a chance to be the center of a lot of excitement--what's the answer? Will the young girl take a chance and swim out and holler for help? Well, X marks the spot where the hollering comes from. The miss enjoys it, the crowd think it's great, and occasionally one of the girls gets her picture in the newspapers and that's just sublime. But these adventures seldom take place on a cloudy Sunday when the beach ain't crowded.

At my swimming pool in Beverly, where once in a while I have to fish a young woman out, I'm having a net made, just like the ones the boys use for seining minnows-- only bigger. I'm fitting it out with a bamboo pole and am just going to snag 'em out. Captain Cox, of the Venice Life Guards, didn't think my seine idea would be popular. "No matter how much the rescuer may think of it," he said, "the rescuee is never going to like it--no struggle--no romance--no beautiful girl lying face upward on the sand--no admiring crowd fighting for a look-see--no allurement--it's out!"

So again I ask: How we going to save 'em when the rip tide gets 'em? Where we going to grab 'em--<u>and be gentlemen</u>!

--Vol. 8, No. 186 (September 3, 1932), page 20.

TECHNOCRACY: THE NEW HOPE

by Upton Sinclair

Note by Ye Ed: Shortly after the filming of The Four Horsemen of the Apocalypse, Señor Ibañez arrived in Los Angeles. We became his host. Of course he would wish to visit the studios. Not at all, but the Missions, ah, yes, the Missions! But whom in this Land of Celebrities did he wish to meet? Only two persons--"Carlos" (Charlie Chaplin) and Upton Sinclair! It is the same with all distinguished authors. Sometimes they may omit the name Chaplin, but never Sinclair. We asked the famous Spanish visitor the reason. "Because we in Europe regard Upton Sinclair as America's greatest living writer. Apparently he is known here merely as a political pamphleteer, but we know him as the author of superb novels of great social significance. I've seen his works translated into every continental language."

In recent years, however, the prophet is gradually becoming honored in his own country.

His novel The Wet Parade has been made into a motion picture by Metro-Goldwyn-Mayer; magazines which were formerly horrified at his political viewpoint and which never would have accepted contributions by him even if such material had been offered, which it probably wasn't, are now inviting him to write for them.

Liberty will soon print a commentary on the recent election from his pen. Perhaps you recall the huge petition, signed by many of our greatest educators, that he be awarded this year's Nobel Prize in Literature.

Thus The Script feels that it has again achieved a notable scoop on other American publications in being the first to print an article by Upton Sinclair on the new and, as he calls it, significant subject of Technocracy. Already other magazines have asked permission to reprint it.

Technocracy: The New Hope   17

Contrary to the general opinion, I have always been extremely
optimistic about my country. I do not like the way it is just
now, but I feel certain that it will change. In my youth I
did a great deal of reading of the history of the Civil War
and the struggle preceding it, and I made note of the fact
that America may seem to be morally and intellectually
dead, and then suddenly awaken and reveal a new soul. I
have looked forward to the same kind of manifestation at the
climax of our present industrial struggle. I have the utmost
contempt for the intellectual insight and the moral character
of the gang which has ruled us for the past twelve years,
but I have clung to the faith that there is a better America,
and that some day we shall hear from it.

Modern Sociology Is an Engineering Problem

Ten or twelve years ago there was formed a group
of engineers and specialists to study our economic problems.
Among the founders of the group were Thorstein Veblen,
perhaps the most brilliant economic mind our country ever
produced, and Charles P. Steinmetz, the electrical wizard
of the General Electric Company. These men called themselves "Technocracy," coining a new word to indicate the
idea that the time of kings and priests and noblemen was
past, and that the time of engineers and scientists was on
the way. They set themselves the task of determining, with
the precision of engineers, exactly how fast the productive
powers of the United States had been increasing since the
beginning, and just what those powers were at the present
day; also what these changes were doing and would do in
future to the business and financial system under which we
live. Columbia University put resources at their disposal,
and for ten years they have been working quietly. Their
task was to assemble exact figures concerning three thousand
industries. They have completed their work concerning eight
hundred, and a couple of months ago they issued the first
report.

The Dawn Comes up Like Thunder

It has been very interesting to me to see the effect
of this document. First there was a brief item sent out by
the Associated Press, and that was all. It was left for an
English editor, A.R. Orage, to take up the document and
make it known on his side of the water. Then, apparently,

the New York editors woke up, and now the New Outlook is publishing a series of articles. The Living Age for December reprints Orage's article, and also one by the director of Technocracy, written in that style which is cultivated by scientists as a means of keeping themselves aloof from the vulgar herd. Now the Illustrated Daily News of Los Angeles has taken up the subject in plain English, and I am told that the messenger boys and bootblacks of our city are eagerly discussing these new revelations--wondering, I suppose, what is going to happen to their professions. In one way or another the facts are becoming known, and it won't be long before the American people realize that here is the most important movement which has shown its head in our time.

Americans Are Science-minded

Socialists have been saying pretty much the same thing for the past two generations; but then, nobody pays much attention to us Socialists. This time, however, it is the leading experts of the engineering professions who are speaking--the sort of people the American public looks up to. What they tell us is that for a hundred thousand years or so men existed on this earth by the power of their own muscles, which meant that society had at its command, expressed in energy values, about two thousand calories per person per day. Then all of a sudden men began inventing machines--first steam and then electrical, and now harnessing the rivers and the tides, and at the present moment it appears that our country has available some billions of horsepower, which means that every American has working for him some thousands of slaves.

A Puzzling Paradox

You would think, then, that everybody in America ought to be wealthy. That is the strange paradox of poverty in the midst of superabundance, about which Socialists like to write and make fables--portraying the man from Mars coming down and asking questions about it, or perhaps an intelligent monkey, or a patient escaped from a lunatic asylum. It is easy to make fun about it, but it is no fun for the twenty-five million people, one-fifth or more of our total population, who must go hungry because they have raised too much wheat, and must go in rags because they have spun too much cloth, and must wander about in the freezing rain because they have built too many houses.

Technocracy: The New Hope   19

A Mechanical Frankenstein

     The engineers of Technocracy show us how it comes about. Every day comes some new invention, or maybe another technical process which increases the productive power of the individual working man, and therefore makes it unnecessary to have so many workers in the factories. Some of the stores which these engineers tell us take our breath away. Yet these are stories of what is actually going on, or would be going on already if it were not that the masters of our machinery are afraid to install the new processes, because already the ones they have in operation are able to produce more goods than can be sold to the impoverished people of our country.

Which Are to Be Slaves--Men or Machines?

     Thirty years ago, it used to be the formula of the Socialists that if the private ownership of the machine were abolished and if we had production for use instead of for private profit, every workingman might have the equivalent of five dollars per day in return for three or four hours' work. How many times the Socialists have been laughed at for making such claims! And how many times have they been challenged to prove it! I remember the crude computations of a Socialist in Austria, Professor Hertzka, in a book called Freeland. But now we do not have to speculate any more, and our old-time dreams are feeble in comparison with reality. The engineers of Technocracy tell us that by working two or three hours a day, we can have a standard of comfort and even luxury ten times as great as we have at present!

We Must Build upon Facts

     But first we have to make these facts real to the public, and we have to get in control of our affairs a set of men who have vision and courage. I am told that more than three years ago, before the panic hit our country, those in charge of Technocracy placed their facts before the Great Engineer in the White House, showing him the way to make real his pledge to the people of two chickens in every pot and two cars in every garage. But, alas, Hoover was not that kind of engineer, and he suppressed the report, and when the panic came he and all his cabinet filled our newspapers with buncombe about prosperity being just around the corner. What Technocracy thinks about that is set forth in two statements: first, that improvements in technical processes during the past three years have been so great that even if we should immediately return to the production of 1929, the work would require only 55% of our labor power; and second, that if the present tendencies continue unchecked, if the policies of bankers and politicians are followed through, in another two years we shall have <u>twenty-four million</u> unemployed to deal with.

<u>Is This to Be "The New Deal"?</u>

We are to have a new president pretty soon, and here is his chance. I am told that his economic adviser, Professor Moley, is one of the Technocracy group. So Roosevelt will hear about it, and we shall see what he will do. I did not vote for him, and I haven't much hope from his administration; but if I find that I am mistaken, and he brings about Industrial Democracy in the United States, no mistaken man will be happier than myself.

What we want is that this enormous industrial machine which we have built up shall be used to produce plenty and comfort for all those who do the useful work, whether of hand or brain.

--Vol. 8, No. 202 (December 24, 1932), pages 1-2

MIZNER THE MAGNIFICENT

by Jim Tully

"Wilson Mizner's death marked the passing of an epoch," said Albert Lewin.

It did. Bill Mizner was indeed the Samuel Johnson of his day, but superior to Johnson in his magnificent sense of humor.

Mizner the Magnificent

I have never known a man who loved life more; and yet, as his doctor brought in a tube of oxygen to ease his last breath, he said to him, "It looks like the main event, Doc." The words symbolized Wilson Mizner's life. He was always a main event fighter.

When I autographed a book for him with the words, "The last of a magnificent school that will soon be closed forever," he looked for a moment, with dim eyes, across Toluca Lake, and said, "Jim, I don't want anyone to feel too sad when school closes for me." Nevertheless, we who loved him will go softly in his great shadow the rest of our days.

Mizner was the Father Confessor to all manner of people who found the way of life strewn with more thorns than roses.

He often covered a sad heart with forced gayety. It is possible the people who loved him never quite knew the real Mizner. That didn't matter. Every facet of his personality was lovable. I recall a remark made by Rupert Hughes some years ago in which he said of a departed friend that she was the wittiest, and therefore the saddest, of women. One who knew Bill Mizner well could appreciate that remark. It could quite properly have been applied to him. He was the saddest man I have ever known. He had early learned that laughter defeated tears.

He once came to my house with Grant Clark, the song writer. Clark had been quite ill and, as a consequence, was very thin. Bill said to him, "When you die, Grant, we'll bury you in a fountain pen." When Grant died, poor Bill was morose for days.

Bill was once the manager of Stanley Ketchell, one of the greatest pugilists that ever lived. When he heard that the brave-hearted fighter was dying, he said quickly, "Count ten over him; then he'll get up."

Bill Mizner was deluged with offers for the story of his life. We, who were close to him, knew he would never write it. We knew what he meant when he said, "You can't write a book with a police whistle."

It might be thought that I am too sentimental about Bill, and that I am trying to paint a picture of a perfect man. If I tried to do this, Bill would roll with laughter down the clouds. Bill had so many faults that his friends just gave up trying to enumerate them. If you made a date with him on Monday, he would show up on Saturday. If he came to your house and got ready to leave, he would just leave. You would look around, and Bill was gone. His faults were his virtues.

But, lest it be thought that I underrate him, he was a man of terrifying reticence and dignity. There were rooms in his tremendous soul which few entered.

Bill weighed about two hundred and fifty pounds. He was the kindest man to food I have ever known. He allowed none of it to go to waste.

He could, and many times did, depict a man's character in a line. He would often say to me, "Jimmy, you're barroom smart."

A younger man than Bill, I was yet close enough to him to travel in his dust.

No other nation could have produced Bill Mizner. O. Henry, Jack London, Richard Harding Davis, David Graham Phillips, Frank Norris--he blended all the finest qualities of these turbulent and brilliant fellows, who are now no more.

I would often call him a lazy man because he didn't write.

He came to my house one rainy night with three gentlemen of whom he said they were "wanted everywhere and welcomed nowhere."

He held a manuscript in his hand, and said, "Jimmy, I am going to read you a story."

The rain slashed at the windows while we listened attentively. I will never forget his gigantic figure as he sat in a leather chair and read aloud the story of high drama on the seas.

When he had finished, I said, "That's a great yarn, Bill. I'll wire Joe Medill Patterson of <u>Liberty</u> about it."

The story followed the telegram, and Patterson wired back, offering a thousand dollars for it. I telephoned the news to Bill, and he complained bitterly, "Lord, Jimmy, it took me eight hours to write that." I said, "Isn't he offering you enough?" "No," was the reply, "He should give me the magazine."

Two years ago Bill came to Reno to cover a prize fight with Mark Kelly, the great sports editor of the Los Angeles <u>Examiner</u>. His first gesture when meeting us boys, who knew the underworld but a trifle less than himself, was, "Now, if anything happens, <u>let me know</u>. I'll fix you up."

That night Bill's own car was stolen! He died without ever getting it back. Often I teased him about it. His reply was, "I'm afraid the loss of that car will bring about a fatal illness."

Bill was a late riser always. He used to brag that he hadn't seen the sun rise since he was two years old. He would always try to get home before the sun came up.

Two men made it possible for him to die in sunlight-- Darryl Zanuck and Jack Warner. They actually induced Bill to go to work. When I condoled with him, in humorous manner, for spending his remaining days at more or less honest labor, I caught the deep misery of his loneliness when he said, "God, Jim, I would work for them for nothing, just to have a place to go." Instead, however, they paid Bill hundreds of dollars a week.

His chivalry to women was that of a thoroughbred. His will is an indication of his tremendous loyalty. He left to Florence Atkinson all that he had. Two women, I am sure, will appreciate this tribute of mine. One will be Anita Loos, and the other, Florence Atkinson. For them the world stood still when he died.

A man who lived in cities, he was a passionate lover of nature. The flight of the bee, the labor of a spider--all these caused Bill to wonder. The man whom H. L. Mencken called the wittiest in America could be silent for long at a time as he watched an ant trudge up a hill with a burden far greater than itself.

Each spring it was Bill's habit to drive into the country and look at almond, peach, and apricot trees in bloom.

His ponderous figure would sag in his car, and the tears would come into his eyes, as he would say, "Lord, Jim, isn't it wonderful?"

April was his favorite month. The reason was simple. It was as changeable as Bill.

Wilson Mizner will not hear the drone of the bees this year--nor watch the buds burst into new bloom. He has gone to another world than ours--where many of his old cronies, and mine, have prepared a place for him. The old rascal will soon have the angels laughing as they fly between the stars.

Bill always loved angels. They made his life easy here upon earth.

--Vol. 9, No. 219 (April 22, 1933), pages 6-7.

GERTRUDE STEIN AND MAE WEST

by Richard Sheridan Ames

The latest phase of the depression is the mental upturn resulting in the popular canonization of two slightly dissimilar ladies, Gertrude Stein and Mae West.

Miss Stein's publishers could hardly have expected her to be runner-up to Faith Baldwin and Ursula Parrott when The Autobiography of Alice B. Toklas embarked. No more certain were the bright boys of Paramount that they had discovered the mother lode or were about to bring in a gusher when they signed Miss West back in 1932 and wondered vaguely what they should do with her.

Both of these ladies qualified originally as Dark Horses. They were cropping in the pastures of neglect or near oblivion, were remembered only by the faithful few, when the gong sounded and they leapt into the sprint for celebrity. The old favorites limped from the start and the girls soon had the field to themselves. Now it's a case of how durable they are--or how much the paying public will stand. The omens are in their favor.

The girls have several qualities in common, though they work in different mediums. La Stein was a pioneer highbrow. She fostered the cult of unintelligibility, was largely expatriate and not noticeably pregnant with sex appeal. La West pandered to lowbrow tastes originally. Her innuendoes were all aimed below the neck, she was as American as corn on the cob and she displayed a hefty load of pulchritude, with or without padding. But they are both wholesome in their brands of fun. They've had to stand a lot of kidding from the sidelines. Both write their own stuff, are seasoned troupers and have an eye for audience reactions.

Since the cinema addresses the populace more directly than the printed word, whose obfuscations increased when subtitles went out, Mae West's public is larger than Gertrude Stein's. Her mots are easier to remember so that millions are muttering. "You can be had" while only the few thousands who buy books are intoning, "Alas a dirty word, alas a dirty third." But Miss West's fans laugh themselves speechless and are in such complete accord over her charms and sallies that they don't argue about her. The proponents of Stein, on the other hand, do nothing but talk; so "Dr. Johnson of Paris" gets plenty of publicity, though she hasn't yet rated the fan magazines or endorsed any soap.

Despite the approval which has made the ascent of these two figures so dazzling, there is a minority element that currently questions their validity in terms of anything except box office. Behind closed doors and strictly sub rosa, the scoffers, whose doubts, publicly uttered, would amount to a conspiracy against the common welfare, have pondered critically the contributions which these two have made to the national arts and letters. Dismissing the plaudits of the multitude as the usual obeisances to the god of ballyhoo, they ask rather indignantly whether they are artists, crusaders, propagandists or the vanguard of the newest crop of Messiahs.

Is Mae West acting when she flaunts, wisecracks, drawls and sings lustily, sporting her bawdy finery of the nineties until the collective libidos of the trousered portion of the audience go tremolo? Is it histrionic art or just what Mata Hari had? Is Gertrude Stein a first-rate poet, critic and prosateur or the Buddha of mumblety-jumblety, the incubator which produced Ernest Hemingway, an official hatchery of the inchoate, the surréalist, the bizarre?

Let us consider the glamorous West, first. When her recent film opened with the usual fanfare in Hollywood, the stars were conspicuous for their absence. Such a phenomenon was unprecedented, since the film galaxy would turn out for anything, from the arrival of Huey Long or Bill Thompson to the Second Coming of Marcel Proust--if there were lights enough. Miss West has a fine record of professional popularity, so the wholesale absences can't be explained by malice or envy. The coast psychologists are still working on the problem.

By her own admission Gertrude Stein couldn't make the <u>Atlantic Monthly</u> until 1933, and even then she was asked to remember what she had learned in composition class, no matter how it hurt her and pleased Mr. Sedgewick. Her works were never best sellers and in the early days their publication was difficult. For years she had endured the almost lethal indifference of the general reader, yet now she is published by the Modern Library and her photograph adorns the cover of a popular magazine.

As the high priestess of a new literary technique she persisted doggedly for years, only to reach her apotheosis at the precise moment when Mae West is enshrined in the notoriously sentimental American heart as a reward for resuscitating the mores, fashions and girdled anatomies of Miss Stein's own girlhood. The <u>dernier cri</u> in literature and a theatrical revival meet on <u>the common</u> ground of almost universal acceptance and mutual popularity--surely a paradox.

But when the countrywide yelping has subsided, when the loud encomiums are hushed and the voice of reason can be heard, we may make some correct appraisal for a curious posterity.

Apart from their artistic attributes both ladies have done some debunking. Mae West rid the American conscience of shame. She made sex funny and sent sin back to the New England cemeteries to slumber eternally with the fanatics who first brought the idea to these virgin shores.

Gertrude Stein debunked herself when she wrote her autobiography. In its pages she emerged--to the popular mind--as a woman, as an innovator who might still be intelligible on occasion, as one who had lived and learned, who had seen through some of the literary myths invented by her adoring apostles. She cleared the atmosphere so that people could read her for what she was worth, and decide for themselves, without critical guidance. Now she has the same fighting chance that broccoli once had in America.

Hollywood fears Mae West, not for herself, but for her influence. When she can do what she does and avoid the intervention of Mr. Hays and the censors, she's guilty of heresy. She threatens the canons of cinema success: tawdry romance, smut and cheap suggestiveness. She's so wholesome that it hurts. Eventually, because of her influence, films that treat of men and women and their relationships may have to rise above the level of a dirty joke.

When that time comes, Mae West may play Mother Goddam and the film will be on the "approved" list of the American Federation of Women's Clubs.

--Vol. 10, No. 251 (December 30, 1933), pages 16-17.

CHARLIE CHAPLIN'S FIRST STORY

My Dear Rob:

I feel I owe you an explanation for not having written a short story for the birthday number of your Script.

At the tender age of nine, even before I was aware of such mystifying things as split infinitives and dangling participles, I was afflicted with that unpardonable ailment known as cacoethes scribendi. In those days my literary aspirations arose from a desire to compete with the authors of those penny weekly "bloods" I had read. It seemed such an easy way to make a living--the sort of thing one could do as homework--in between times, as it were.

I remember I had several ideas, as I thought, but on reflection, they were not ideas--they were merely "lead-offs." For example:

"Bang, bang, a shot rang out in the misty night as Bill Carstairs fled from the bridge and secreted himself beneath the dank arches, where he breathlessly waited, hoping against hope, to evade his pursuers...." And that's as far as I could get.

Another inspiration was as follows:

"A scream rent the midnight air--it seemed to come from the old empty house that stood at the corner of West Square. John Harkaway, a young barrister, stopped abruptly--rooted in amazement...."

Again my boyish inspiration dried up. Since those days, my literary projects have seldom gone much further than a first paragraph; with perhaps one exception, the article I wrote for the Woman's Home Companion, which I eventually completed, and which, I might add, was a supreme task for a cove like meself.

And now, after all these years, you come into my life and ask me to write a short story as though it were a mere dip of the pen.

Nevertheless, in all seriousness, I have an idea for a story which I might write some day. It is about an eminent scientist who has discovered a genuine cure for all disease--the news of which brings patients, humble and rich alike, from every part of the world.

In developing the story I shall describe the thousands in their pilgrimage to the clinic. There are millionaires, scientists, men of great prominence--all clamouring to be the first to receive treatment. Many patients wait for months and some die before being admitted.

I shall describe the professor as a man of unusual charm--a whimsical character who cares neither for money nor fame. He is a poet and a philosopher, with a sense of values somewhat disturbing to the world at large.

He issues a statement that all patients wishing to be treated will be considered first according to the importance of their service to society, and not according to their financial status nor the prominence of their position. This creates a great deal of controversy. The press and the populace proclaim that the men of science should receive the first consideration, but the professor will not hear of it. He maintains that the most important of his patients is not the scientist, but the poet. He must come first, and the rest shall follow, conforming to the category in which he places them.

His edict, of course, creates great indignation. Even his young assistant takes issue with him, but the professor is resolute--nothing can change his decision.

At this point in the story I shall develop a Platonic dialogue between the young assistant and the professor. I shall have them sitting in the dusk in a comfortable apartment overlooking the roofs and chimney stacks of the great metropolis.

"How can you possibly place the poet above the scientist?" argues the assistant. "What poetry can compare with the contribution that science has made to humanity? Take yourself for example,--you have conquered disease and prolonged life. Isn't that more important to society than all the sing-song abstractions of the poet?"

I shall write a charming description of the twinkle-eyed old professor calmly smiling and smoking his pipe.

"Prolonging life," says the professor, "is not very important. It will probably lead to overpopulation--then famine and death will follow in spite of all the scientists. Ah, my lad, longevity is not measured by time. It is in the imagination of man. The poet can live an eternity in a moment and the fool but a moment in all eternity."

"But why should poets come first?" persists the assistant.

"Because they are the source and spring of all inspiration; they are the high priests of the soul, who preach the gospel of beauty; they write the text books of all civilizations and lay the foundations of our desires. They make men want to live for more than bread alone. Their dreams are beyond dreams--their desires beyond desires. The scientists are merely dabblers in speed, the makers of gilded beds upon which we never rest--the promoters of luxuries which we seldom enjoy. No, my boy, the poets are first, for they sing through the darkness of the ages, while the rest of us grope blindly, their songs our only guidance to lead us on and out into the sun."

This is an idea for a short story, but I am afraid it will never be written.

Regretfully yours,
Charlie

--Vol. 11, No. 258 (February 17, 1934), page 8.

FRANK CAPRA

by Jim Tully

His eyes always wide open, as if he were listening to a startling story, and was about to ask, "Is that so?"

He is an Italian, coming to this country when he was three years old.

Forced by the exigencies of circumstances to learn all the commercial aspects of directing for the box office, he has, and this is to me the greatest wonder, become an artist.

I like to think of him in connection with his Italian contemporary, Frank Borzage. Both are great technicians. In their highest moments, they are spontaneous, emotional.

No master of words, not even Thackeray, knew the thin line between sentimentality and pathos, so well as Frank Borzage. And not even Mark Twain could have handled gusto with more adept spontaneity than did Frank Capra when he made those seat-worn passengers of a Southern bus spring alive with song in It Happened One Night. And what is more, he borrowed Clark Gable from M-G-M and made him a charming light comedian.

The story is one which not even a cinema critic could believe. But it is also one which the most tired cynic would like to believe. Like Lady for a Day, it is as impossible as honor among politicians, but one finds oneself transported for the time in which it unrolls on the screen. And that, to me, is the essence of romance.

Frank Capra is still growing. The technical shackles of Mack Sennett are still upon him. But not even technique can completely thwart an innately great intuitive artist.

In a long acquaintance with people of the films, I am still amazed at the vast number of them who have known early hardship. Capra sold newspapers on the streets at five years of age. He was graduated as a chemical engineer from the California Institute of Technology in 1918.

During the years which intervened, he touched life at more angles than a criminal lawyer. He had a long boyhood struggle with poverty--he was a student of Rob Wagner in Manual Arts High School, where he worked his way by, of all things, playing the banjo, upon which he is a skilled performer. He worked as a waiter while going through the California Institute. He edited the college paper on the side. This did not keep him busy enough, so he earned money at other employment with which to help the folks at home.

These experiences were bound to mark deeply a lad born with considerable mental and spiritual capacity.

Right after graduating from college he became a second lieutenant in the Coast Artillery during the war to make the world safe for depression.

Discharged after thirteen months, he wandered the streets of Los Angeles looking for a job. For six months he wore the army uniform, until it shone like an office general's. Like a dumb girl's virtue, it was all he had.

A morbidly sensitive fellow, his experience at this time brought about an illness, more mental than physical. An understanding doctor jerked him out of this condition, and once more the future director was on his way. And it was too bad--for his next job was that of trimming trees in the San Fernando valley--at twenty cents a tree. He lived in a shack--and wrote short stories at night.

This enabled him to buy some new clothes, and after lending his uniform to a major, he obtained a position as private tutor to Anita Baldwin's son.

An advertisement for scenarios whetted his attention. He came to Los Angeles and went to work for a "honky-tonk" director and producer. For the next several years he learned a great deal about picture making.

Eight months passed in which he was gag man for Hal Roach in the "Our Gang" comedies. He was next with Mack Sennett for two years in the same capacity.

Then Harry Langdon branched out in feature films, and took Frank Capra with him. This was eight years ago. Capra directed Langdon in The Strong Man. It was chosen as one of the ten best pictures of 1926. He has since continued to do very well for himself and the business which he adorns.

His contract with Columbia Pictures is for three years, and said to be unique, in that it is not cancellable during that time. But who the devil would want to cancel his contract at any time? Surely not so dynamic and keen a showman as Harry Cohn.

Capra is still under forty years of age.

No man now directing is his superior in the element of surprise and the human touch. The man who wrote the short stories in the San Fernando valley shack would have become an excellent craftsman had he continued in the business of letters.

After the preview of It Happened One Night he said to me, "Some day a musical comedy will be made on the screen, and it will all be as spontaneous as the singing in that coach." He referred to one of the best film scenes of the year, one which I have already mentioned. There is a thinking brain behind what seems to be such natural spontaneity in Capra. He is the intuitive craftsman under control.

Frank Capra as a man, is capable of high laughter and compassion. In his jaw is determination, and in his eyes is pity. He can tell a yarn and bend an elbow with any man. If he has ego, it is like everything else about him-- definitely under control.

Being human, he is pleased with praise, if it is sincere.

But his eyes open no wider when his work is criticized.

On his way to far places, is the lad from the farm in Italy.

> --Vol. 11, No. 260 (March 3, 1934), page 12.

LOS ANGELES--A PAIN IN THE NECK TO NEW YORK

by Don Herold

Los Angeles is a thorn in the side of New York. Los Angeles is not aware of this, and would not worry about it if she were, because Los Angeles does not worry about anything.

Now, New York is similarly annoyed by no other city in America. As a rule, New York either dismisses all other cities with a sniff, or manfully admits their merits up to a certain point. Philadelphia is merely a big, sleepy settlement where they shoot mail carriers. Boston is a backward village where they censor the work of New York novelists and playwrights, a bothersome habit, but one sometimes quite helpful to the publishing and theatrical business.

Chicago has good crime, good corruption, plenty of dirt in more senses than one, a metropolitan roar and a cobble-stone rattle, grime, dinginess, smoke, ugliness and beauty, undeniable industrial viciousness, a certain literary activity which serves at least as a kindergarten for New York's literary ranks, and an art school which produces many of New York's illustrators. Thus Chicago, for these several reasons, wins a modicum of New York's respect.

Detroit has a verve, and, if nothing else, produces automobiles, which New Yorkers love. Palm Beach and Miami are merely resort towns, designed entirely for the convenience of New Yorkers. New Orleans is an old-world city which many New Yorkers hope to visit because it is Old-World. And San Francisco's reported metropolitanism is something which New Yorkers would like to investigate some day if San Francisco were not in the same state with Los Angeles. Los Angeles alone, of all American cities, irritates New York.

New York's eyes are on Europe. New York worships Paris and London, and it is extremely disturbing to have Los Angeles tugging at its coat tails like the child of some poor relation. If the average New Yorker contemplates a trip, it is eastward, not westward. New Yorkers most respected by their fellows are those who have been to Europe innumerable times, but who have never been west of the Hudson river.

Of course, the man in New York's subway is not harassed by Los Angeles; he has too many counter-irritations; to him even movies are made in Heaven. But the articulate classes (and when you speak of the thought or feeling of any city you have to speak primarily of the thought and feeling of those persons in the city who have thought and feeling, and who can articulate it and who make a fuss, probably an exaggerated fuss, about it--writers, critics, artists in all fields, actors, dramatists, conversationalists, intellectual windbags)--these citizens of New York are given a pain in the neck by the very existence of Los Angeles.

Eventually, Los Angeles orders most of them to come to Los Angeles on some chore, as a desperate housewife calls a plumber, and with about as much respect; but whether these persons ever go to Los Angeles or not, they hate Los Angeles. They look down on Los Angeles every time they go to a movie and see the things Los Angeles is doing, and every time they read a novel and contemplate what Los Angeles will do with it in movie form, and every time they go to their sacred theater and imagine Los Angeles' debauchery of the play when it makes the movie version, and every time they look at a magazine or newspaper in which Los Angeles is mentioned (which is pretty frequently in late years).

As long as possible they make their contacts with Los Angeles through agents, and get most of their impressions of the place through acquaintances who have journeyed out there to have their sensibilities outraged and their purses flattered. Eventually they themselves get an offer or are overcome with curiosity or get a nip of sinus trouble or a cough or high blood pressure or incipient anemia or a nervous breakdown, and go out to the godawful place in person.

Their suffering is amusing to those of us who have been through the mill and come out alive. (It never kills, fortunately.)

At the start, when they do go out, Los Angeles usually drives them to drink, and they join with fellow exiles in wild parties, and one of their first impressions is that everybody in the place is drunk all the time. "People drink hard out here," they say. The moving picture industry is a gigantic shock to them and the city of Los Angeles is a violent depressant. They come out expecting powerful vulgarity in the screen world and hick manifestations in the huge village of Los Angeles, and they are disappointed in neither of their expectations. If they come as picture employees, they are no doubt allowed to sit idle for weeks, or are otherwise wasted and violated.

One of the first legends they hear is of the writer who went to Europe for two months and was not missed, and who drew his check each week through his agent, and who came back to resign and was told by the studio executive that what he needed was a change of viewpoint and a rest and who suggested a trip to Europe at the studio's expense.

Los Angeles' booster boastings have reached New Yorkers' ears even in New York, and they now find themselves rubbing elbows with the most virulent civic pluggers in the world. The whole town seems to have eaten hops. "A new super-race is springing up here in the Southwest," writes the oracle of the Los Angeles Times.

Climate consciousness is almost a perversion and climate conversation is a passionate indoor pastime.

Real estate is God. Hollywood is the self-acknowledged style center of the world. Will Hays has told Los Angeles (and the rest of the cockeyed world as well) that Los Angeles is setting cultural standards for the universe, and Los Angeles believes it. New gas stations are opened with searchlights sweeping the heavens, a symphony orchestra, and movie stars in attendance. Grocery clerks wear artists' smocks, and barbers dress as if for an abdominal operation. Waitresses are in opera comique garb. Vegetable markets have palatial grandeur. Cerise Rolls Royces roll the streets.

A movie opening is a veritable cosmic orgasm, with a hundred searchlights scorching the sky, and the populace lined up for a mile on either side of the theater, for hours before and after the performance, to adulate its cinematic gods. There is talk of naming public schools after Bebe Daniels, Richard Dix, Gary Cooper and other stars. Guides drive at a funeral pace past the house of Tom Mix and whisper that it is the home of Buster Keaton.

Rantings of religious cults reach the newcomer's ear. He may subject himself to the depressing experience of attending one of Aimee McPherson's shows and of watching this extraordinary actress cast her spell over a group of the most broken, submissive, susceptible humans ever gathered into one temple. He sees medical quackery rampant, and hundreds of private residences with neon signs out as sanitariums and cures. Dog and cat hospitals of grand proportions dot the city. Wilshire Boulevard is sometimes spoken of as the Fifth Avenue of the West, or, more likely, Fifth Avenue is referred to as the Wilshire Boulevard of the East. A certain section of Wilshire is advertised as the Miracle Mile.

Hot dog stands are palatial. Flower shops are shaped like flower pots, coffee stands are shaped like coffee pots, with steam puffing from the spout, ice cream stands are huge ice cream freezers. There is a theater called "The Million Dollar." Yachts are on sale in vacant lots. (Strange that Don didn't call attention to our fountain of Peterless Pans! But p'rhaps he's in favor of sterilizing surgery, even on statuary. --Ye Ed.)

Local intellectuals mispronounce their big words. At an adjoining table in the town's finest cafés, you are apt to find a party with half its members in evening clothes and the other half in open-collared sport shirts, sweaters and knickers. Six-thousand-dollar Packards stand in front of four-thousand-dollar bungalows. Your next door neighbor may have four hundred thousand dollars, and wash his own Pierce-Arrow and dry the dinner dishes for his wife, to save a maid.

An Indian octogenarian, reputed to be worth fifty million, stands on the corner of Wilshire and Vine and amuses himself by directing traffic at certain hours of the day. Men's clothes are more violently patterned and men's shoes are yellower and wider-toed than anywhere else in the world.

Los Angeles--A Pain in the Neck to New York

All these things, the New Yorker observes the first few weeks he is in Los Angeles.

He observes the movie industry to be manned, to considerable extent at least, by a type which seems to be a cross between a big city racketeer and the most naive Middle-West rube. Here New York pants-makers and Illinois street-carnival grifters join in the promulgation of a new art. He sees a country population gone giddy with an impulse to entertain the world--and itself.

He sees toothpicks employed openly, and false teeth taken out and shaken to emphasize a conversational point. Two-acre cafeterias with forty-piece orchestras attract thousands of tipsavers and lovers of food-in-quantity.

If he rents or buys a house, his doorbell is besieged by an endless stream of cranks, petty merchandisers and mendicants.

He sees the world's greatest collection of phony candy-box architecture and the fanciest imaginable line of stucco flavors from strawberry to pumpkin. Theater exteriors and interiors of California maniac school.

Filipinos in college-kut clothes.

Women's culture clubs of gargantuan proportions. Breakfast clubs where sedate members must address each other as "Hello, Ham," and answer, "Howdy, Egg!"

He says, "What is there to do at night except get drunk? There are no theaters. No night clubs. Let's have some highballs."

No wonder that in a few weeks he is ready for a straightjacket. He hates Los Angeles, and in most cases out of ten goes abruptly back to New York and tells how.

It's an interesting transcontinental phenomenon. And it is happening often enough now to warrant recording.

Your outraged New Yorker overlooks the fact that this is (probably) not the first time in his life he has lived in the country. He fails to admit to himself that he is merely rejoining a peasantry he left when he deserted Bucyrus, Ohio, in 1916 to make his name and fortune in New York City.

For fifteen years or more he has been living in a city of
European immigrants, and he has now, as a friend of mine
once soothingly reminded me, transferred himself to a city
of American immigrants.

    As immigrant or steerage classes go, they are really
a better bunch. Our transplanted New Yorker's pain is
partly due to a subconscious unacknowledged realization that
he has been forced back to the farm. He thought he was
through with country life forever, and he wanted to be through
with it, yet here he is back again among country folk. Well,
that is not so terribly serious, if he would only name the
disease.

    And he forgets what a pain (intermixed with thrills)
New York gave him (if he was any good) the first year or two
after he moved to New York. The vulgarities of New York
can match fairly well the vulgarities of almost any other
place in this country. Peasant smells are a little stronger
in the subway than almost anywhere I know. He forgets the
torn newspapers blowing among the dust on New York streets.
He forgets how he used to look for human-looking people
among the crowds even on Fifth Avenue. (Even Fifth Avenue
traffic presents about one "hot number" to the lineal block,
if you stop to scrutinize it critically.) He forgets how often
he used to swear and avow in New York traffic jams that he
was through with theater-going forever. He forgets the
tediousness of New York's picture palace prologues, with
their almost impromptu glow-worm ballets, and with music-
box figures coming to life, and all the old stuff. He forgets
the depressing crassness and coldness which he though New
Yorkers had, the first few months he lived there. And the
cattle effect he saw in people catching their cars, and in the
garment trades out milling on the sidewalk for the lunch hour.
He forgets that there is hardly any spectacle, even in Los
Angeles, as rural as a first night in the New York theater,
with its claque and exhibitionism. He forgets that he wished
many times, during his first months in New York, that he
were back in good old Bucyrus, where there was a certain
freshness and cleanliness and friendliness in life. He forgets
that he had to become acclimated to the peculiar offensive-
ness of New York.

    He should allow every town its shortcomings.

    But it is probable that he flies back to New York before
he has weathered Los Angeles, and once back in New York he

Los Angeles--A Pain in the Neck to New York   39

adds his voice to the hymn of hate that New York has for
Los Angeles.

    I, personally, have been through it, and I now happen
to live in both towns, back and forth, and to like certain things
in both of them. Not that I have any desire to evangelize
Los Angeles to New York. I find it quite necessary, and
about equally necessary, in either, to anesthetize large
blocks of my consciousness.

    The New Yorker transplanted to Los Angeles may in a
year or so learn to like the place, if he will relax, and deliberately develop several blind spots. It may or may not
be worth the effort. He may have to quit reading some of
the more rabidly local local newspapers or to skip certain
of their columns automatically. He can learn how to stay
away from quarters in which boosters congregate, and he can
drive past the fanciest filling stations and patronize those
which merely sell gasoline and oil and which do not insist
on wiping his spectacles or cleaning his scarf with naphtha,
gratis. He can learn how to stifle climate talk (unless, in
fact, he, himself, comes to enjoy a mild climate epicureanism,
which is perhaps no crime in the eyes of God, who, let us
remind Californians, made climate). He can learn to deal
curt insults where they will do the most good.

    He can learn to stay home from banquets where they
may discuss "our beloved California." And he will come to
enjoy living outdoors, and stepping out into a garden instead
of into an elevator, and he will learn that it is just as entertaining to go round the corner to a fairly good seven-thirty
movie and get home before ten o'clock as it is to fight one's
way to and from a third-rate play in New York City, a half
of which it is impossible to hear on account of bronchitis
which that lousy climate back there seems to induce. (Yes,
he will even find himself talking like this.)

    He will develop a sense for the six or eight good
things which come to the theaters each season, even in Los
Angeles. He will perhaps enjoy athletic events which thrive
in a town with two big rival universities and a sports-loving
populace. He will read more. He will require less tension.
He may enjoy decent health for the first time in years--carnal,
but true. He will find that if he goes to New York a week or
so in the spring he may see the six or eight plays of the
season which have been good enough to last that long, and that
he may thus spare himself the suffering of attending a winterful

of flops. His nasal lining will feel less like suede, and he will breathe a lower percentage of monoxide. He will find for himself a legitimate M.D. and a barber who will not use the clippers half way up his skull.

In time he will find a group of friends who have lived many places, perhaps even in New York, and who have relaxed even to the torture of living in Los Angeles--fine, philosophical souls who can take this punishment lightly, and who have their laugh at the climate, and who belong to no culture clubs, and who know the movie industry for what it is worth, and who mix bicarbonate of soda and witchcraft in about the proper proportions in curing their ailments. Frequent trips will lessen the distance between New York and Los Angeles, and he may even find himself traveling in Europe in Sabbatical years. (There are usually more persons in Europe from California than from any other state in the Union, I believe.) He will enjoy seeing his children run in and out of the house and playing outdoors in light clothes a good many days of the year, though he will frankly admit that it gets pretty darned damp and pretty darned cold some of the time, even if it is California, and that it is a mistake to build or buy a house in California without an adequate heating system.

If he ripens into the complete adult that travel should make of a man, he will become just as annoyed at and just as tolerant of the New Yorker who is cracked on New York as at and of the Californian who is cracked on California.

He won't go visit New York and rant or complain and he won't come back to Los Angeles and rant or complain.

And, for one thing, he'll get a much larger kick out of going to New York than he got out of living there all the time. He may even come to believe that New York is a swell place to visit but no place to live--and thus, when he mentions it in New York, feed further New York's hate for Los Angeles.

Cities, love one another; you're all bad enough!

--Vol. 11, No. 266 (April 14, 1934), pages 6-7 and 25-27.

NOCTURNE

by Charlie Chaplin

Beneath an oak
  Beside a lake
Through shimmering lace
  I see a moon.
And silver notes
  Of mirrored stars
Trill upon a resonant pool.

The distant rhythmic mountain
  ranges
Symphonize the unknown theme,
Man's destination--
  Why and Where
  Eternal Truth
The Real; the Dream.

Across the sky
  An eagle high
Conducts the silent symphony.

                  --Vol. 12, No. 292 (November 10, 1934), page 3.

SO HE DIED LAUGHING
A Funny Story Dedicated to Charlie Chaplin

by William Saroyan

On the seventh day of his misery he began to laugh. It began in the morning before breakfast, although there would be no breakfast anyway, while he was walking along Main Street in front of the cheap clothing stores, the cheap restaurants, the cheap burlesque houses (the opium of the people is everything which is nothing which is finally late at night in the foul-smelling theater Lily Rafe herself in person a configuration of woman slyly uncovering her magnificent breasts to the blood-moan-melody of <u>Miss Otis Regrets</u>), the cheap burlesque houses, admission 20c, this laughter, on the seventh day, walking in the morning among the weariest of a weary race, in the weariest of a weary age; this race, the highly-advertised American, and this age, the tin-can age, also the cinema age, also the ranting age: now, 1935, March, the day Thursday, the time morning, the one who walks yourself.

And he walked with this laughter, tipping his hat now and then to the lamp-post for amusement.

The laughter was quiet and wise, inward and ancient and not really his own; it was the mouths of all dead of the earth twisting with his mouth to the fierce wisdom of pain and death, and it meant this: <u>this</u> is idiocy and insanity. These hard streets of rock, these hard walls, these dark and sullen holes within the walls, within the city, where they rest and wait and sleep: these shapes of life, the gray torn masks of town, the night-haunted eyes, the bodies of crumbling bone. The foul state of life.

So he laughed. Sure. He knew: the universe is the way you feel; sometimes you feel good, sometimes you don't, and you always feel lousy when your money (whose money?) is ending and you've had no decent food for seven days and you look like hell and you can't get a job (even though you have the diploma) and you won't beg, and your patience is ending, and all you can think is: Well, this is very funny because this is myself and if I'm not careful I guess my goose is cooked and I guess maybe I won't be alive this time next spring, I'll be dead, whatever that is, I'll be rotted into the top floor of the Chrysler Tower in Manhattan, I'll be the bright boy whose soul saved the universe because he died laughing.

Sure. It was himself, only it was everybody too. It was everything, every tragic atom of the cockeyed universe, every agonized electron of matter everywhere, animate or inanimate, including God Himself (poor fellow), or if that couldn't be, the next best thing: the dictator of Germany, or the dictator of Russia, or the one of Italy, or the one of America, anybody important on a horse or in a Packard or on a platform or before a microphone, ranting, shouting

So He Died Laughing

jitney philosophy: Comrades, brothers, lovers of opera, patriots, students, slaves and idiots, tax-payers, fellow-countrymen, believe, and you will have bread to eat and wine to drink, and in time you will love forever.

In Pittsburgh.

And even if you don't believe that isn't going to stop the grass from growing, and if you suddenly find yourself dead, your body sprawled up a dark alley, your face cold with the weary mirth of life and death, even that isn't going to stop the coming of spring next year, and sometimes in the plains of the Mid-west there were moments of unmistakable magnificence of life, as when you breathed, standing upon the levelness of the earth, and walked, and drank water, and ate bread, and said impudently, God Almighty, I live and by Jesus I can never die.

And of course there was no place to go: nowhere to take the laughter and have it heard. Here is a young bloke in a cheap suit who says he's got something important. What is it? Well, it's laughter. He's probably nuts. Gentlemen, he would have to reply, this is the whole business: the opium of the people is the universe. I have the greatest gag of all time: and the answer is yes. Gentlemen, the only thing to do is laugh.

And they'd lead him to the big brass door, and open it, and say to him, Scram, punk, that gag's the oldest known to man or beast: it stinks. And the Communists would say, Comrade Harper, 21, graduate of the University of Kansas, was brutally murdered last night by the Capitalist system, so he laughed and walked nowhere, going up and down Main Street between the Court House Building and the slums below Pico.

He walked all day and half the night, and then, since there was nothing else to do and nowhere to go, he somewhat died, laughing. Actually, though, he simply went on walking, carrying the banner, beginning somewhere in time and the universe and the street of the world, to live forever, which is never, and for an eternity the substance of his flesh stumbled through the dark city and the spirit of it sank into the earth and everywhere in space was the sound of his laughter, loud, but no louder than silence.

--Vol. 13, No. 313 (April 6, 1935), page 4.

OR LEAVE A KISS WITHIN THE CUP

by William Saroyan

It was dinner and the restaurant was all right, not too flashy, a Greek place with the clean Greek smell and the sporty Greek headwaiter, and it was the little, tired waitress trying to be gay, bringing with her two Scotch and sodas, two crab cocktails, two consommes, two salads, two filets, rare, two coffees, two pieces of pie, and it was fine, it was dinner, it was eating food at night and being alive, it was talking to Irma at the table, it was the world, the amazing sadness of the world, and it was saying to her, You can never tell, maybe it is true: maybe they will kill Hitler before summer and then everything will be all right.

It was talking quietly about Hitler from the small booth in the Greek restaurant.

Maybe they will kill Mussolini, too, he said. I guess maybe they will kill all them bastards.

He sipped the Scotch and looked at her, the sad quiet shadow of her face, the sad sealed lips, the sad eyes, the sad smiling.

I'll ask the waitress, he said.

They won't kill anybody, said the girl.

I known they won't, he said, only I like to believe Hitler will be dead by summer.

And the thick glass ash-tray was very sad, and the tall sad glass of Scotch, and the sad salt and pepper shakers with their sad shadows, and the sad people in the next booth, and the sad street outside, and the sad buildings, the sad windows and doors and halls and rooms.

Hitler is a rat, he said. He is a major rat. Nobody minds a minor rat.

The waitress came with coffee and pie.

Or Leave a Kiss Within the Cup   45

You ought to know, he said to the waitress. Is Hitler a rat, or isn't he?

The waitress looked at Irma and understood. It was joking. She wouldn't lose her job or anything.

I'll say he's a rat, she laughed.

You see? he said to Irma. Everybody knows Hitler is a rat. The whole world is waiting for Hitler to die. Nobody will be happy again till Hitler is dead.

The waitress went away smiling to herself, but not altogether unbewildered.

They'll think you're crazy, said Irma.

No, he said. Everybody is secretly hoping Hitler will be dead by summer.

It was sitting at the table and talking like a fool because he loved Irma. It was wanting everybody young and alive to be unhindered by Hitler and the other rats.

From the Greek restaurant they went to a movie. It was a lousy movie, and the idea was to prove that love and love alone is what the world is seeking. So it was a good movie, too. You could tell how much of it was lousy: the rest of it was good: it was people in clothes wanting to be naked together, so it was good. There was a lot of trouble, but the idea was for the man and the lady to step out of all the artifice and falsity of civilization and be naked together. This part of the idea wasn't greatly stressed in the movie, but you could tell what the idea was, anyway. Every man, woman, and child in the theater was in favor of the idea. Everybody thought it was an excellent idea.

It was Saturday night and they could sleep till noon Sunday, and they had worked all week, so they were in no hurry to get home, and they went to a quiet little democratic beer joint, no orchestra and no fuss, just beer and a table, and they drank beer till two in the morning.

A little after one in the morning a young Italian came to the place with an accordion and began to play. He was a very sad-looking Italian and the music he played was very sad. He wasn't altogether blind, but he couldn't see very well.

When he played certain passages of music he would lose himself in the music and his face would be full of all the love-sadness of the Italian race. He played "O Sole Mio" and "A Vuchella," and you knew it wasn't the Italian race, it was Mussolini.

    Irma was a little drunk and he himself was a little drunk, but it was all right, it was music, "O Sole Mio," my sun, Italy, simple people singing of love, it was the whole world in sadness, wanting love, and every time he sipped beer Irma sipped beer and this was part of their love, part of their innocence together, part of their kinship, to be awake together, in a little beer joint, drinking beer together, hearing the sad music of the young Italian together, being alive in the world together, in the same place, each of them one of millions, each unknown, yet unlost, each fixed in time and the universe because of love, and it was splendid, and within the cup was the kiss, and they drank to one another with their eyes, and he knew they were drunk and immortal, and he believed firmly that Hitler and all the other major rats would be dead by summer and everything would be all right again in the world.

                                --Vol. 13, No. 315 (April 20, 1935), page 6.

WILL ROGERS

by Rob Wagner

The Fool is dead! Long live the... No. One may exclaim thus in regard to Kings. But not Fools. The King attains his status by the simple law of primogeniture--his father was King before him. But Great Fools are not born of Fools. They are what biologists call "sports"--oddities--the breakers of Mendel's law of heredity. There is no Mendelian accounting for the World's Great Fools--Cervantes, Shakespeare, Benjamin Franklin, Mark Twain, Charlie Chaplin or Will Rogers--all humorists and philosophers, the combination that makes the Magnificent Fool. <u>Their</u> parents were Time and Circumstance.

Cervantes was born at the twilight of the Age of Chivalry. And he kidded it out of existence. Shakespeare was the ripened flower of the Renaissance when the world was aflame not only with the new discoveries of distant lands but the art of printing. Ben Franklin proved that even an ambassador could be allowed a sense of humor and his own printing press permitted the spread of this happy discovery. Mark Twain appeared at a time when the printed word could be multiplied tremendously. Chaplin arriving at the birth of a new art form, carried his Foolishness even to those who could not read.

All the World His Stage

But of all this army of noble Fools, Will Rogers enjoyed the widest field of expression--the rostrum, the printed word (not crystallized in books just for the few, but in daily newspapers for the multitude), motion pictures and radio. No man of the present generation has had so huge an audience. And no man has ever so completely won their affections. We had hoped to write our humble appreciation of Will Rogers, but the avalanche of tributes to his heart, mind and spirit that appeared the day following his tragic death has overwhelmed us. We could never have written paragraphs so poignant as those of Harry Carr in the *Times*. Nor could we even hope to express such a poetic thought as this from the pen of Rupert Hughes:

> "He made the world ache with laughter when it was most needed. The hearts of those who loved him should rather rejoice than ache. Seeing that, since all must die, our laughing philosopher went like a medieval magician on winged adventure to die like a falling star at the edge of the Polar Sea."

Behind the Arras

But we can tell of some things regarding Will's work that are not generally known. His artistry, for instance--art that concealed art. People attending his lectures, banquet speeches, reading his column or listening to him on the radio gained from his casual manner that all his witticisms and philosophic epigrams were spontaneous and simply burbled forth without previous thought or preparation. True, his effervescent mind continually struck brilliant sparks on the instant but his major premise and its collateral witticisms were carefully thought out in advance. In other words Will was not only the greatest humorist of our time but a superb artist with a finely studied technique which he carefully concealed by an assumption of bashfulness and casualness. All this we learned by an intimate association with him both as director of his comedies and as a fellow writer.

Recognizing His Limitations

When Will began writing for the Saturday Evening Post he was genuinely bewildered. He could talk his stuff, but the printed word--except in short paragraphs--was new to him. So we would go up to his house while he read his piece to us. Knowing that he wanted the truth and not flattery, we would explain that while his local witticisms were terribly funny the piece as a whole lacked construction and a strong central thread upon which to string his pearls. He would screw up his face and look as serious as a Mayan sculpture. But he'd go to work on the idea. It was the same way in preparing our film stories. So effervescent were his wits that he'd be off and away in all directions with bright ideas--grand, but another story. Recently he said to us, "Rob, stories are not my game. I've got so now I don't try to horn in; these studio fellows know their stuff and now I just go out and do what they say."

The Confession of an Artist

Not so with his lectures and banquet talks. One day we asked him if they were as spontaneous as they sounded. "No," he answered, "my lectures are shows. I'm puttin' on an act. Of course I mustn't let 'em know that, but my embarrassment and gum chewin' are part of it. I have a series of routines carefully thought out and if I see that one of 'em is dyin' on me, I shift to another. I know exactly what I'm goin' go say when I go out. I read the local papers and by talkin' to folks, frame up some good local gags, but the lecture as a whole is an act. When I was in vaudeville I could always turn to my rope if I felt my talk routine was floppin'. It gave me a chance to collect my wits." All of which is the frank confession of an artist.

Curiously enough, though Will loved to contact people, he liked his lectures least of all his professional stunts.

After a series of short-reel comedies in which the studio insisted that he clown like a red-nosed comic, he gave up in disgust. "Rob," he said, "I'm going out on a new lecture tour and I can't tell you how I hate it. But I've got to."
He expressed the same hard-working conscientiousness when we asked him why he was always on the go. (This was after his return from flying all over South America.) "I do it to get material. If I stayed in one place all the time I'd go stale." Nor was his greatest interest in motion pictures. Best of all he liked reporting and comment.

Know Thyself!

Will's greatness was also evidenced by his being fully aware of his limitations. While he understood men and had a curious psychic understanding of events, he had had no training in the intricacies of government. Yet there were always "movements" to catapult him into practical politics. The fact that Beverly Hills elected him "Mayor" (a grand and honorary joke because legally, as a city of the sixth class, we couldn't have a mayor!) stirred the politicians to use him in their game. Several years ago a bunch of frockcoats waited upon us. They had a great scheme. "Rogers for President!" The boom to start from Claremore, Oklahoma, and Beverly Hills, California, his two homes. We were to father the plan in Beverly Hills.

Without mentioning the matter to Will, we came out in an editorial laughing at the idea. We said that Will's greatest strength was on the sidelines of the passing show. And that should he run for office he would immediately lose half his audience. We further explained that he was not equipped for such a position. That he knew little of academic questions and that the intricacies of a finance or tariff bill would utterly bewilder him. It was a nervy and perhaps impertinent thing to write and Will never mentioned the matter to us. But we got word indirectly that Will approved and was pleased to be relieved of the embarrassment of having to refuse nomination for "the greatest gift from the hands of the American people."

Bread on the Waters

But of all Will Rogers' qualities his greatest was his Christ-like spirit of giving. He gave of his heart, mind,

talents and purse. Naturally the world was at his gate.
True, his protectors finally had to lock the gate to his Santa
Monica ranch. But he told all and sundry just where the big
key hung! We were out there one day when a woman came
trudging across the lawn--a mile up from the road. How she
got in nobody knew. But she went away with a handful of bills.
On another occasion a committee arrived from Oklahoma to
invite Will to speak at some sort of anniversary. Will was
tied up with a picture, but he went down into his jeans for
enough money to pay for their railroad trip.

    The same with his time. One evening late we drove
out to his place (yes, we knew where the key hung). The
servant said Mrs. Rogers had gone to bed and that Mr.
Rogers was upstairs writing his piece for the papers and
had asked not to be disturbed. But Will had heard our
voices and came shuffling down the stairs. We protested
and told him to go back to work, that we had to go on anyway. "There isn't anybody I'd rather see than you folks,"
he grinned. And with that he entertained us for an hour or
more--giving of his rich and happy spirit. Every time we'd
start to leave he'd say, "No, now, just wait a minute, sit
down--sit down...." It was our last visit with him.

The Last "Spot"

    Yes, Will's life was one of giving. And it was this
impulse that led him into far and dangerous places. "I
haven't much brains," he once told Ye Real Ed, "but what
I have I juggle around to the best advantage." And so, still
in search of material and to recharge his restless spirit, he
juggled them over the precipice.

    One night at the Writers' Club Robert Cromie of
Vancouver delivered a lecture using a huge map of the world.
After the lecture Will, fascinated by the map, went up and
began to point out the spots where he had been. They included about everything this side of the Arctic Circle. Apparently that was the one place he hadn't seen. So when Wiley
Post invited him on that dangerous venture he simply couldn't
refuse.

    Indeed, so great was his output that his urgency for
new ideas kept driving him on and on. Then there was also
his Indian blood. Like his Cherokee ancestors he was brave
and venturesome, and always wanted to know what was on

the other side of the mountain. Now, bless his precious spirit, he <u>knows</u>!

The newspapers are already searching for another Fool--one to pick up Will's cap and bells. They may find one to fill his <u>space</u>, but they'll find no one to fill his <u>place</u>. There never will nor can be another Will Rogers. He was unique in Time and Circumstance.

--Vol. 13, No. 329 (August 24, 1935), pages 1-2.

BOY O BOY O BOY, O BOY

by William Saroyan

He guessed he knew what they were trying to do, the big fat-heads. They were trying to scare him, so he would stop yelling so loud. Mulligan the traffic cop, and Tommy the bar-keep, and Schultz, the jeweler. Well, he'd show them. They wanted him to go away from the corner and let the neighborhood have a little peace. They claimed he made more noise than a dozen newsboys. Well, maybe he did. So what? Wasn't he supposed to let them know what was going on in the world? Wasn't it his business to let everybody know how Mussolini was making out in Africa? They were sore, he guessed, because he was an Italian. Well, so what? Sure he was. And a good one too. A spaghetti-bender, and if they didn't like it, well, they could take it up with the government.

Mulligan wasn't really a bad guy, he had a heart of gold, only he thought he was funny, making cracks about the Italian army. Hey, wop, he said, how's it going with the army, hey?

Plenty good, that's how, he said. (Mulligan was a guy who was always smiling and if it came to trouble Mulligan would be scared out of his wits: he was nothing but an old cop who got a big kick out of holding the hands of little kids and walking across the street with them.)

Ha ha, he said, and how's it going with the big flat-feet, Mulligan?

Ha ha ha, and he ran like hell.

Boy O boy O boy, O boy, was old Mulligan sore at him? Boy, was Mulligan mad?

Well, it served him right making cracks about Mussolini's army in Africa.

And a mighty swell army too, if you asked him. All young Italian kids from Naples and Sicily and Rome and everywhere else. All good spaghetti-benders.

And Tommy, the little fat-bellied bar-keep of The Shamrock Inn. Tommy wasn't a mean guy, only he was just like Mulligan, he liked to shoot off his mouth. How come, he said, you're yelling so loud these days, kid? How come you ain't taking it slow and easy the way you used to before the Italians started killing the Ethiopians?

Well, I'll tell you, he said to Tommy. Between you and me, it's because I'm a wop, see? (Tommy wasn't much, and he really liked the little fat-bellied bar-keep, but he didn't like the spirit of all them gags.) And that ain't all, he said. Who the hell do you think you are? You're Irish, ain't you? Well, I guess maybe Ireland has troubles too. I guess maybe the English sit on you babies once in a while.

And boy O boy O boy, O boy, did that burn up Tommy? Did that make Tommy sore?

Well, they had it coming, the wise guys. Making cracks at him and Mussolini.

And the jeweler Schultz. Abe, the jeweler, the little loud-mouthed Jew with the small white hands, always monkey around with little tiny watches and rings and bracelets and that kind of stuff. Who cared about that little guy? What could he do? Acting tough. Coming around and showing him a little machine, maybe the inside of a clock, and telling him it was a sound-detector. Telling him just as soon as the little machine showed that he was yelling too loud, Schultz would inform the police and have him sent up to San Quentin for life.

For what? he asked Schultz.

For winning the African war, said Schultz. That's what for.

I ain't yelling any louder than I always yelled, he told Schultz.

Like fun you ain't, said Schultz. This machine don't lie. You been making more noise around here than all the rest of the people in the neighborhood put together.

I got to sell my papers, he told Schultz.

You don't care about selling papers, Schultz said. All you want to do is let everybody know Italy is winning the war. That's all.

(And Schultz was right; that was the worst of it. That was all he wanted to do. He just wanted everybody to know Italy was Italy, and boy O boy, the Italian army was some army.)

Oh, yeah? he said to Schultz. Well, how about you, Mr. Schultz? How about the way you got all excited when Hitler started the rough stuff in Germany against the Jews. I suppose you didn't go around acting like a crazy man. No, not much you didn't. You made more fuss around here than I'm making.

And boy O boy O boy, O boy, did that get the best of Abie? Did that make Abie blink his little eyes and look mad?

Trying to scare him and make fun of him. Well, they couldn't do it.

Mussolini wanted to take real care of all them poor Ethiopians in Abyssinia, that's all he wanted. He wanted a few other things too, but he was going to give all them poor people shoes and bathtubs and telephones. He was going to teach them to build modern houses, and Mussolini was going to put electricity in the houses and washing-machines and vacuum cleaners, and he was going to build schools and teach everybody to read and write, and he was going to do everything. Benito Mussolini was going to do everything, and he'd like to see anybody in the world stop Benito

Mussolini. We eat spaghetti and drink red wine, he thought. We fill our stomachs and that makes us want to do stuff in the world. There's lots of room in the world for Italians, north, south, east, west, and everywhere. Columbus went to hell and gone and reached America, and Columbus was a wop, wasn't he? So what the hell were they making cracks for? Benito Mussolini was a great man, that's what for. Everybody was jealous of Benito Mussolini. The King of England was jealous. The Dictator of Russia was jealous. Adolf Hitler was jealous. He guessed everybody in the world was jealous.

He was pretty scared, all the same.

He could see old Mulligan standing in the street, blowing his whistle and holding out his arm, and waving at the cars to go or stop.

Mulligan looked pretty sore at the world. His poor old feet were tired, he guessed.

He passed in front of The Shamrock Inn, and didn't go in. He used to go in and sell papers to the guys who were getting tight. Now he was scared to go in because he knew Tommy was sore at him.

And he saw Abe Schultz in the window of his little store, looking out.

They were all sore at him.

Well, that was all right too. What could they do? He was supposed to sell his papers, and that's what he was doing. He was yelling the headline every afternoon, and he was yelling it loud, so what? He was happy about everything, and he'd like to see anybody stop him, or stop Benito Mussolini, away over there in Rome.

One afternoon two colored boys walked by his corner, and Boy O boy, they heard him yelling about the war. Boy O boy, they turned around and looked at him, and his heart started running wild, and he said, All right, if they want to fight, I'll fight. I'd like to see anybody stop Mussolini from teaching them people to read and write. If they're looking for trouble, all right. I won't run; but he wasn't so sure.

One of the boys was a little bigger than he was, maybe fourteen years old, and the other was about his own age, thirteen.

They looked like brothers, and the next day he saw them again, and he noticed the way they looked at him, as if they didn't enjoy the racket he was making.

He was pretty scared. The two colored boys started laughing just when he began to feel really scared, and boy O boy, the way they laughed, real loud, the way all Negroes laugh. Real strong, making fun of everybody. Laughing, telling everybody they didn't care. Go ahead, do anything you want to do. That's what scared him most, the way them two colored boys laughed. It spoiled everything. All of a sudden he didn't feel like yelling. He didn't feel like opening his mouth at all. All of a sudden he started feeling sorry about Benito Mussolini. He was still hearing the colored boys laughing. He was still seeing their black faces, their big mouths opened by mirth and indifference, their big white teeth flashing.

There was something about them people, the black ones of the world; the easy-going way they had, moving around slowly, taking it easy, laughing out loud. Maybe they didn't need to learn to read and write. Maybe they didn't need modern houses with electricity and washing-machines and vacuum cleaners and all that other stuff. Maybe they got a kick out of just being alive, hanging around, doing nothing much, just laughing and being somewhere or other. That was the worst of it, and it made him feel sorry about Benito Mussolini. What's the use? he thought.

What's the use bothering all them black people? What's the use teaching them stuff they don't need to know? What's the use taking all them young Italian boys out of Naples and Sicily and Rome and making them shoot at them big Negroes? What good did it do you?

Mulligan noticed the difference a half hour later; the kid wasn't yelling at all. What the hell was wrong?

And on his way home Tommy the bar-keep noticed that the little wop wasn't yelling.

And Schultz noticed it, too.

That's too bad, Schultz thought; we were having so much fun, kidding him.

Mulligan stopped at the cigar stand on the corner the next day to buy a couple of nickel cigars and find out who won the fifth at Bay Meadows. He saw the kid standing on the corner, looking like an orphan in the world, and not yelling.

Hey, wop, he called out, what's eating you, anyway? Why ain't you yelling about the Italian army? Anything wrong?

The boy turned around and looked up at the big traffic-cop. He didn't know what to say. What could you do about them black people, anyway? They had everything. They laughed and let it go at that. They were wise. He wanted to tell Mulligan just how he felt, but he couldn't think of the right words and the right mood to go with the words.

Anything wrong? he said to Mulligan. I'll say nothing's wrong. We took Makale yesterday, and we're getting closer to Addis Ababa every day. I'd like to see anybody stop Mussolini's army. Boy O boy O boy, O boy.

And he started hollering louder than ever.

--Vol. 15, No. 344 (December 7, 1935), pages 4 and 6.

HOW TO BE A WRITER

by William Saroyan

You walk first away from the ocean, or east. Then you turn suddenly and walk toward the ocean, or west. The ocean will be discussed later. What it means and how going to it will help you to write. It is part of the ritual to walk first away from the ocean, because if you walk immediately toward it, your prose is apt to be too difficult for average tastes. It is always preferable to hem and haw awhile along the way, taking your time, yawning, and greeting the neighbors, local, alien,

How to Be a Writer 57

or universal. It is, at any rate, excellent calisthenics to walk in the direction of the place you do not intend ultimately to reach and it helps a lot to fill space, making seventy thousand words appear where seven would have been enough. It is also good discipline. It is not good art to write as the crow flies, and it is useful to study the habits of the various rodents that dwell two or three feet below the surface of the earth. The darkness will be identified as Russian, the structure as French, and the activity as a combination of both, with a dash of American.

The important thing is to go through one day at a time, one moment at a time, smoking one cigarette at a time, being alive and yawning. Rules for sleep are not to be discussed in this treatise, but it is not to be supposed that the serious writer of prose can by any means come to ignore the fundamental importance of this matter.

Briefly, it is advisable to sleep with your head toward the south pole.

The question of whom to sleep with cannot be discussed here, but it is contrary to no federal or state law to name people not to sleep with. Social workers are always preferable for not sleeping with, and dazzling debutantes come second. Ladies who write love stories are very fine ladies not to sleep with, and countesses are splendid people to smoke cigarettes with.

The ocean to be discussed here is the Pacific. Its magnitude has never before been related to the great body of world literature, but this has been due to the fact that almost all our writers of the past have been largely interested in grammar and punctuation, and not due to the fact that the Pacific Ocean is not the greatest single force in English literature or the noblest tradition in any literature.

A brisk walk to the Pacific Ocean will sharpen the dullest writer's grammar and improve the finest stylist's rhetoric. It is one of the best known ways to begin a short story about unemployed stock and bond salesmen, ex-multimillionaires, ex-Presidents, and the public. The admirable and advantageous thing about the Pacific is that it combines the best features of mobility and immobility, and that anyone is privileged to appear in its presence without having to pay admission, and without being taxed. It remains one of the few large things that clever writers have not been able to punctuate, isolate, stylize, remove, beautify, or violate. It is there, the Pacific, and a brisk walk each morning to it is one of the things a good writer must perform.

Another important rule is to be English. Any other race will do, but to be English is to be among fine people. If one is not English, however, it is always courageous to make contributions to the language introducing into it as much of silence as possible.

There are several other rules, but they are boring. The most important rule, according to everybody, is to run like hell after the money. It helps to prolong the manufacture of automobiles.

Several important don'ts are:

Don't be a Communist, Capitalist, Democrat, Republican, or genius. Don't write for posterity; there is no such thing. Don't write for editors or publishers.

The slickest rule of all, however, is: Don't write. I will gladly teach anyone the fundamentals of not writing. There is no cost, no obligation. You don't even have to clip a coupon. All you have to do is think it over carefully.

--Vol. 15, No. 371 (June 13, 1936), page 20.

CRAZY HOLLYWOOD
A Letter to the Communist Scenario Writers
Hollywood, Calif. March 21, 1936

by William Saroyan

Comrades and Fellow workers. It ain't the money, it's the principle of the thing.

I get an idea for a colossal movie every day except Sundays and Jewish holidays. At writing every variety of dialogue I am ninety-nine and nine-tenths per cent supreme.

Crazy Hollywood

Nobody in America knows more about hokum than I do. I'm a natural for Hollywood.

I ought to be lousy with money. I ought to own a Packard. I ought to be a terrific force in the industry. Well, Comrades, I'm down here in Hollywood. I'm stopping at a cheap hotel, a block and half down from Hollywood Boulevard, three blocks up from Vine.

This town is lousy with Comrades who are lousy with money, who own Packards, who have servants, who are terrific forces in the industry. I'm a Comrade myself, but I ain't in on any of the big dough. Hollywood doesn't want to do business with me.

In the first place, I want plenty of money: $20,000 for an idea. Wow.

Take the one I got this morning when I got up and couldn't find a new blade to shave with.

It's colossal:

A fellow who's worked hard all his life for twenty dollars a week or less wakes up one morning and steps out of a furnished room without a window into the heavenly world once dreamed by Karl Marx, but long since forgotten, especially by students of dialectical materialism, Comrades, and racketeers. Everything in the world is jake at last: no errors, no waste, no disproportion, equilibrium everywhere, balance everywhere, grace, laughter, delight, health, and so on.

That's the idea.

I got it this morning when I couldn't find a new blade and had to shave with the blade I used yesterday to sharpen pencils with. If it isn't worth $20,000 of Metro-Goldwyn-Mayer's money, it isn't worth a penny. Of course there isn't enough love interest in it to make a part for Harlow, but even so, it's a colossal idea, which, if properly developed, would be a great box office hit.

The young worker is dead of course.

When he steps out of that rat-hole into the magic world of Karl Marx, it's not really him, it's his poor ghost, the tragic shadow of his over-worked, under-nourished flesh.

That's what I like about the story. The poor bastard's dead. The poor fellow has wakened into perfection. He's joined God and Marx.

I got this supercolossal idea this morning, and I rushed right out into the streets of Hollywood, badly shaved, and began telling people about it, on account of I ain't dead yet, and on account of the world is still the world, the foul-smelling dump the other side of the railroad tracks of the universe.

I wanted people to know about this idea.

I told it to the Jewish newsboy from Brooklyn who wants to be an actor.

Fritz, I said. Look. A poor bastard who's worked hard all his life like a lousy slave wakes up one morning and steps out of his furnished room into a perfect world. It's a movie, Fritz. The poor bastard's dead. Catch on? He steps out of that rat-hole into death, peace on earth, good will to men. Ain't it colossal? I'm going to sell it to Thalberg for $20,000, not a penny less. How do you like it, comrade?

It's lousy, he said.

So I bought a paper.

You're a sucker, Fritz, I said. How do you figure it's lousy?

The guy's dead, he said.

You're a dope, Fritz, I said. You're nuts. Look. You want to be an actor, don't you?

Yeah.

You're ten times as good as Cagney, ain't you?

Yeah.

You're tough, ain't you? Really tough, no Hollywood honey.

Yeah.

Well, look, you'll be an actor in the movies when you step out of the same lousy furnished room. Get the idea? This is a story of every crazy overworked undernourished sucker in the world.

It's lousy, he said.

So I bought another paper and went away.

What makes you Comrades think the people are with Karl Marx? How do you figure? Let me tell you who the people are with. They're with Hearst, Democracy, Individualism, The American Magazine, and Idiocy. They're gaga. And let me tell you another thing, Comrades. Let me tell you who the class-conscious babies are with. Class-conscious my nut. They're with Paramount, Metro-Goldwyn-Mayer, Warner Brothers, Fox, Columbia, and Universal.

Well, push my right eye out, what are they doing there?

Are they changing the world from the garbage dump to the garden? Are they making the dialectical dream come true?

Well, no. They're okay, good Communists. They're writing movies, Hollywood movies, and they're collecting plenty of money for doing it.

Not me, though. I'm in this lousy hotel, and I'm in debt. I ain't got any money and I need money. I could use some of this Hollywood money. I've got more poor relatives than any other writer in America. Then why in hell don't I be a good boy and sell out like the other Comrades? I'm good. Everybody knows I'm good even if I do brag a lot. I can get a good job writing for the movies in ten minutes if I feel like taking the proper attitude.

Then why in hell don't I?

Well, I'll tell you.

It's because I'm one of the best radicals in this country. Not a Communist, not a patriot, but a good crazy radical. I believe in everything. I believe in God and the people. I have all the faith in the world in the under-nourished and overworked, the weary and diseased and haunted. I think something can still be done about them. I think they can be fed, rested, healed, made whole again. I'm that crazy. And I think no force in the world can begin to feed and heal them like the force inherent in the moving picture. I believe in the moving picture as a force capable of awakening the people, instead of putting them to sleep. There's no religion in this country, and no opium of the people, except the moving picture of our day, and the good Comrades are writing a lot of these moving picture stories.

I'm in favor of moving pictures. I want to help bring about the making of the kind that ought to be made. I'm not getting a thousand a week for adapting a crappy <u>Saturday Evening Post</u> story. I'm saying. Here is an art-form which has come into being inevitably, and must be accepted by the most serious artists of our day. Here is the only art-form of our day, of our time, our life, and we've got to use it as effectively and as nobly as serious artists have always sought to use any other art-form. Here is the world's tongue. It's dumb now, but it's capable of speech.

The moving picture is okay and don't ever kid yourself that it isn't. It's plenty okay. It is the only instrument of expression and criticism capable of keeping up with, and interpreting the flux of, our time. We can be proud of the moving picture.

So let me tell you well-informed Proletarians something very important: namely, that if Karl Marx were alive today, he'd be jumping around all over the place telling you dopey babies what to do with the moving picture, what it is your <u>obligation</u> to do. He'd have a fifty-thousand word chapter on the subject. He wouldn't let you guys get by with selling out to Paramount, writing horse crap and missing the whole point. He'd ride the asses off of you. He'd have you excommunicated. So maybe it's a good thing he's dead and his book is closed. You're lucky he ain't around anywhere, and you're lucky nobody else like him is around. You're radical all right, but I think if Karl Marx were alive, he'd be raising hell with you boys. So you're waiting for the revolution, and you're writing Hollywood movies?

It's going to be a fine revolution, in the dark theatre, in the sick brains of the people.

That's a gag. That's a colossal movie too. Maybe I'll write it some day.

THE UNKNOWN SOLDIER SPEAKS

by Eddie Cantor

Oh God, if the Nazis only knew
That I, their Unknown Soldier, am a Jew!

They pass my tomb and salute with pride:
They who made my mother a suicide.

What is left of my heart cries out in vain
At my brothers' torture--the endless pain.

Fathers and mothers, daughters and sons,
Souls put on the rack of these Godless Huns.

Take off this iron cross, and before they die,
Give it to my people; they deserve it, more than I.

Oh God, when will this persecution cease,
So once again I can rest in peace?

Look--here comes their leader to
Lay a wreath upon the tomb of a Jew!

FASCISMO AMERICANO

by Philip Dunne

It is hard to understand why the American people, so passionately averse to Communism, have lost little sleep over the possibility of a Fascist dictatorship in this country. We reject it categorically as impossible, unthinkable in America; it is so utterly foreign, so opposed to our own sweet ideal of liberty.

Communism is a much more obvious menace, admittedly boring from within, permeating our factories, our schools, even penetrating to that sacred institution known as the American home! Red-hunting has become a national sport. But the chase is not as exhilarating as we have been led to expect. The Communist may be a tiger in Russia, but he's a rabbit in the United States. Rabbits become a pest only when they can multiply freely, and our Communists have not multiplied. Their annual electoral registration is pitifully small.

But we pursue the rabbit merrily, and in doing so we have wandered into the forest of a tiger so ferocious as to make the Communistic feline look like a tabby-cat. He is stalking us today. Most of us have never seen him, for he has a highly protective coloration. Only once has he showed his stripes, and that was when the Black Legion was exposed. But this was a mere twitching of the tail of American Fascism. It is the head that contains the teeth, and it is the head which is hardest to see, because it blends so subtly into the American landscape.

There are three types of American Fascist. The first is the out-and-out Black Legionnaire, or White Crusader, or whatever he wants to call himself. He is a part of the tail. He is the potential Storm Trooper, the lad to wield the bludgeon and administer the castor oil. He is not numerous. If you put an admittedly Fascist ticket in the field for this election, it would make an even punier showing than the Communist ticket.

Fascismo Americano

The second is the typical member of the so-called "lunatic fringe"; the man who will follow any posturing and grimacing leader with a crackpot scheme to share the wealth. He is decent, honest but bewildered. He means no harm. He is merely hard up. But he is blood brother to the decent, honest, bewildered, hard-up German who helped Big Business put Hitler in power. When simple Hans found out what he had done he naturally grew querulous, and was promptly, to use the quaint Nazi idiom, "purged." It was an expensive lesson.

The third type is the most dangerous of all. Dangerous because he is the most numerous, and doubly dangerous because he hasn't got the remotest idea that he is a potential Fascist. In fact, he denounces Fascism with almost as much soul and vigor as he denounces Communism. He is the American business man, or preacher, or lawyer, or farmer, or carpenter, or Legionairy who so rejoices in his four-square, red-blooded Americanism that he does not realize that this Americanism itself is being used as Fascist propaganda. He reads inflammatory editorials in our pro-Fascist press, and unctuously repeats them to us. The ringing phrases sound daily in our ears: "Labor unions are controlled by Communist propagandists.... Big Business is the savior of the nation ... all liberals take their orders from Moscow ... save America for the Americans." Always the Flag, waved in our faces until it no longer resembles the familiar symbol of our free democracy, but becomes an alien and tawdry piece of bunting, like the Nazi swastika, or the fasces of Italy.

"The last recourse of a scoundrel is patriotism." Never was that quotation truer than it is today. Patriotism is the life and soul of Fascist propaganda, and it is good propaganda, because it is emotional. Mussolini invented it; Hitler uses it with superb skill; unscrupulous Americans are employing it today. And it works. It works so well that countless Americans have had the wits charmed clear out of their skulls.

On a recent trip to New York, I met an aggravated case. He is an immensely rich man, an able lawyer who has twice held high public office. He is known, and respected, as a gentleman, a sportsman, and an unstinting philanthropist. He told me that 90 per cent of the American people were morons, that the intelligent 10 per cent should take over the government, abolish the vote, and use the moron majority in the fields and factories as they, the 10 per cent, saw fit. He identified the 10 per cent as the "most successful" (i.e. richest) Americans today. He admitted that for a while it would be necessary to use the Army and Navy to put down the inevitable insurrections, but insisted that the people would receive so many benefits that they would soon cease to object to the loss of their democracy. (Presumably as they have ceased to object in Germany and Italy!) Somewhat shocked, I pointed out that what he advocated was Fascism. At this, he blew up. Nothing of the sort! It was nothing more nor less than good, common sense, Jeffersonian Americanism! He explained that Americanism only survives today among the favored 10 per cent, the moronic ninety having been thoroughly infected with Communist ideas, spread among them by Jewish propagandists. (Note the final, revealing touch.)

Later, in a club dining-room, I retailed the gist of this extraordinary conversation to other prominent citizens. But, instead of indignation or outright laughter, I aroused only head-shakings, mutterings that "perhaps the philanthropist was right; after all, you know, you can't trust the people too far; hope it doesn't come to that, of course, but there is a lot of loose Communist talk going 'round, and-- well ...."

I went away from there understanding why some liberals go off the deep end and embrace Communism outright.

What chance do we run of seeing an American Fascist state? A very slight one, if our voters keep their heads. But the tiger is in the woods, large, vicious and artfully concealed by patriotic platitudes.

The motive is there. Anti-laborites are indignant enough over the progressive policies of the Roosevelt Administration. The Liberals are in the saddle and our potential Fascists are howling for Mr. Roosevelt's blood. (With cynical irony, they even accuse him of having set up a Fascist dictatorship, which would make him the first Fascist to boast of the 100 per cent support of Fascism's moral enemy-- organized labor.)

The Fascist organizers are ready for action, backed by wealth and armed with the bigotry and intolerance of many of our people.

Fascismo Americano   67

But as yet there is no <u>duce</u>, no <u>führer</u> to mesmerize the voters, no Personality Boy-extraordinary to cook up the elaborate vaudeville act which sells Fascism to the people.

Ninety per cent of the American Fascists will support Governor Landon, but that does not mean that Landon is the Duce. He is not. He is an honest Old Guard Republican of the Harding-Coolidge-Hoover line. If he were elected and really tried to return to the horse-and-buggy methods of his predecessors, he might be forced into Fascism by indignant labor; but he isn't the type to make a success of a course which would be abhorrent to him.

Huey Long is dead. His spirit goes marching on, clothed--somewhat shabbily--in the flesh of the Rev. Gerald Smith. The Rev. Gerald exhibits all the symptoms of Fascism, but somehow lacks the magnetism of your genuine <u>duce</u>. Or does he? We must not forget that ten short years ago, Hitler was considered a ludicrous and unimportant political figure, even in Germany.

Father Coughlin is even more raucous than Smith, a finished rabble-rouser in the best Fascist tradition. But he is a Catholic priest, in name if not in practice, and that, politically, is the finish of him.

American Fascism will get nowhere without a dictator. Somewhere he exists; somewhere in the murky valleys of politics lurks the American Hitler. Soon or late, he will appear. Let us pray that when he comes, he will have the mark of the beast set on his brow, so we shall know him.

--Vol. 16, No. 378 (August 29, 1936), pages 8-9.

THE END OF THE WORLD

by William Saroyan

<u>Kyrie Eleison,</u> said the priest.

Kyrie Eleison, answered the clerk.

Kyrie Eleison, said the priest again.

Christe Eleison, said the Clerk.

Christe Eleison, answered the priest.

Christe Eleison, said the clerk again.

Et cum spiritu tuo, said the clerk.

Then he removed the massbook and knelt at the altar.

The priest said:

Dominus vobiscum.

Et cum spiritu tuo, answered the clerk.

    The clerk was a young man of eighteen. The priest was a short old man of sixty or so who was growing fat and listless. The priest went through the mass as if he didn't have much faith in what he was doing, but the clerk served him humbly and with energy, giving the priest wine and water, preparing the basin and cloth, removing the basin and cloth when the priest had washed and dried his hands, kneeling and moving about, crying out humbly yet passionately the Latin words he had memorized but did not understand. The young man felt, nevertheless, that he was saying words of some importance and certainly of great dignity. *Et cum spiritu tuo,* he cried with youthful passion, and the priest felt dimly, this boy is an ox: he bellows; he does not chant.

    It was James Giordano. He was a new clerk at St. Anne's. He came from somewhere in the North Beach, and seemed to be a more than normally serious young man. The priest thought he would have a little talk with the boy some time soon and find out why he was so serious. Some of the Irish boys who served the priest were no less efficient than James Giordano, and yet they were more amusing to have around. They made him feel there was still liveliness and mischief in the living, and even when they forgot their lines or said them wrong or out of place, he didn't mind, and on the contrary smiled to himself, keeping all the while, a most pious face.

The End of the World   69

The boy almost ran into the church only an evening later, and he was almost out of breath when he found the priest.

Father, he said, I want to talk to you. I don't want to confess because I haven't had any new sins since last confession. I only want to talk to somebody.

The priest walked with him out of the church. It was a clear winter evening.

And I want to talk to you, the priest said. We will take a little walk together.

They walked down Nineteenth Avenue toward the park.

Something is troubling you, the priest said.

Yes, Father, said the boy.

What is it, my boy? said the priest.

Father, I have visions.

Visions? cried the priest. What do you mean?

And he thought: Now I begin to understand. I know these young men. Night and day they think of only one thing, and the serious ones are worse than the others. And in his mind he saw the young man dreaming all day and night of the great body of woman, the gigantic female of the instincts, maddening and evil and yet magnificent. He would talk to the boy quietly. Find yourself a good companion, he would say. The Lord created you to share your life with another. There is no evil in love.

And rather than pity the boy, the priest envied him. Which way of life is holier than the simple and innocent way? he wondered. Unknowing, and in ignorance, they achieve godliness.

They walked in the park. The tall eucalyptus trees made deep shadows and the stillness was soothing to the priest. It was good to be walking beside a young man, one who would soon enter life in all its fulness.

Tell me what you see, said the priest.

Father, said the boy, I see the world ending. For weeks now I have been seeing the end of the world. I am not frightened, but I want to talk to you.

This angered the priest because he was a man of little faith, and he did not believe it was possible for an ignorant young man, an Italian, to have such a terrible and glorious vision.

What happens? he said.

Father, said the boy, everything ends. The cities burn and fall, and the living die.

What nonsense, thought the priest.

I thought I ought to tell you, the boy said.

Well, said the priest, it is because you are young. There is nothing to fear.

Father, said the boy. He was very anxious.

Father, he said, I am not afraid for myself. I am prepared to die. I am afraid for the others who are not prepared, the worldful of them. They do not know. I thought I ought to tell you. I see the world ending all the time. When I close my eyes to sleep I see everything ending, and when I open my eyes I see all the people dying. I thought I ought to tell somebody.

The priest took the boy by the arm.

It is nothing, he said.

Nothing? the boy said.

It is all right, the priest said.

The boy did not understand. Father, he said, I see them dying. I thought somebody ought to tell them.

How old are you? the priest said.

I am eighteen, Father.

Have you a job?

Yes, Father. I am a waiter at the Fior D'Italia on Broadway.

Have you had a loss recently?

A loss, Father?

Has someone dear to you passed away? Your mother or father, a sister or a brother?

No, Father, they are all alive.

Have you a girl?

A girl, Father?

Are you in love?

No, Father.

I thought so, the priest thought.

He believed he had reached the bottom of the whole thing, and was quite pleased.

It is nothing, he said. There are many nice girls in the church, he said.

What shall I do, Father?

Find a good girl, the priest said.

Father, he said, do you mean that I should find a girl and tell her about the vision? Do you mean I should tell only one person to be prepared? Not all of them?

Good Lord, the priest thought.

Why do you feel you must tell everybody about the vision? he said.

I see the world ending, Father, he said. I see everybody dying, Father.

Everyone alive will some day leave his mortal flesh, the priest said.

This dying is not the same, Father, the boy said. They go on moving around the same as ever, but there is death in them. I cannot explain it, Father. I see them dying all the time, and they will die.

Nonsense, the priest thought. What shall I tell him? he wondered.

Oh, he said.

What shall I do? the boy said.

The priest himself wanted to know what he should do. The boy was certainly in earnest. He was certainly seeing the world ending and the living dying. He was not anyone sly or mischievous. He was not playing a joke.

The priest wondered what he would do if he were eighteen and very ignorant and very faithful and had visions of the world ending and the living dying. It would be a very awkward experience, to say the least.

There is nothing to do, he said. You must be patient, and I think it would be very nice if you found a good Catholic girl.

They walked together in silence out of the park. The priest was not altogether pleased with himself because he knew the boy's vision was no common thing. If the truth were known, it was a most remarkable thing. But good Lord what could he do about it? What could anyone do about it?

In the street the young man said, I thought I ought to tell you, Father.

You did right in telling me, the priest said.

I will be patient, the boy said.

That's right, the priest said.

I will find a good Catholic girl, Father, the boy said.

I think that would be very nice, the priest said.

Good night, Father, the boy said.

Good night, the priest said.

And that was all. But walking away from the boy, the priest was deeply troubled, deeply angry with himself, but even more deeply jealous of the boy. Who was he, a boy of eighteen, to have such a vision? It was really too ridiculous.

--Vol. 16, No. 391 (November 28, 1936), pages 4 and 6.

NIGGER: SAYING GOOD-BY

by Dore Schary

He stood there, his left hand raised in a gesture of farewell. The fingers gripped a torn, dirty cap. Slowly the hand fell to his side. His right hand held a worn suitcase tied with a strong piece of twine to hold in the baggy, thin fabric that bellied with the garments packed inside.

The sun grinned down on his gleaming ebony face.

The valley stretched below him, green with spring; the air was rich with new blossoms and the trees waved their leaves in happy rhythm.

Saul stood there--his heart heavy in his thin chest.

He stood there--lonely and aching. There had been twenty springs before this one. Twenty springs, green, alive and fragrant. Only last year he lay on this very hill and felt the soft grass beneath his hard back; looked at the turquoise sky and the shifting clouds.

It was beautiful then--beautiful now. But different.

Last year Mammy and Pap had been there. Pap plowed that field and sang as the earth rolled away from the sharp plowshare. Mammy had been in the shack near that clump of oaks, and on the stove had been pots and kettles full of cooking good for hungry men.

It had been like that for years--happy years of work and ambition. Plant--harvest--sell and buy. Buy another acre--buy more of an earthy happiness--buy another patch of brown ground and blue sky. Pap used to tell Saul that was the nigger's salvation--to buy the ground below and the sky above--'cause God threw in the stars, sun and moon for nothing.

Sometimes at night Pap would tell them the most wonderful tales. They'd all be sitting on the steps or stretched out on the cool earth. Mom would stand in the doorway looking out--she always looked so tall and straight standing there. And in her eyes were a softness and a tenderness that always made Saul feel like crying. But Pap would talk and the others would listen. Saul and Bess and Jim would listen. Bess, holding her rag doll close to her tan cheek, would look at Pap with wonder in her eyes. Jim, strong, handsome Jim, with the wide smile and powerful chest, would chew and listen and sometimes he'd talk of places he'd want to visit. Places he'd read about in the school books. And Pap, wise Pap, would tell them that the world was here--here in this lovely valley. Because here was happiness and the world could offer no more. And then maybe they'd all sing.

And when the moon sank behind the silo they'd all start in to the house. Soon the sun would be brightening the dark and quiet night and there was sleep to be had--sleep so needed for the glorious tomorrow when the earth beckoned again.

Saul stood there on the hill and saw it all. But this was another spring. He bowed his head in pain when another memory crept in and pushed out the sun and the moon and the stars and the singing.

He remembered that night. The night of the rain. The heavens, black with water, poured out their burden on the land. Pap, Mammy, Bess, Jim and he had listened to the drumbeats of the rain on the wooden roof. It was some rain, the biggest he'd ever seen, reckoned Pap.

The biggest rain in years. Big enough to tear down buildings--wash away bridges--uproot husky trees--pull down silos and push everything before its angry way. The levees had cracked and the water swept into the valley.

Nigger: Saying Good-By

There was a rending, racking groan as the water hit the house. Bess screamed. Jim, knocked senseless by a falling beam, lay stretched across the cold stove. Mammy had grabbed hold of Bess' arm, and Pappy, his eyes wide, met the crash with a troubled, bewildered look.

The flood swept them all away. It carried Saul to a safe refuge in the sturdy limbs of an ancient tree.

But the rest were gone. Gone to a dizzy, choking death.

The sky was here--the sun, the moon, the stars and even the earth was here. New earth--green--fresh and gay. The floods were gone. It was a new year.

New levees ready for the next flood. Yes, and new people working the ground bought from the bank.

New plows--new horses--

Saul lifted his head.

No Pap in the shade of the oak--no Jim--no Bess--no Mammy. No anybody.

Turn your back, Saul. Drink the salt of your tears. Eat the lead in your stomach. Somewhere in the hills beyond are other green pastures.

"Yes," thought Saul, "it's a new life and I wish I was older--I'm too young. Got to wait too long to see everybody."

He turned and walked down to the road and started away.

A gust of wind blew the dust about his feet and a wretched sob heaved his body.

"Goo'-by," he said, "goo'-by."

--Vol. 16, No. 392 (December 5, 1936), pages 8-9.

OUTLINE OF ECCENTRICITY

by Irving Wallace

Ever since the Great War, eccentricity has been on the wane. In far corners of the globe may still be found a few members of the dying order, stifled by a world stuffy with sanity, to wit: Dizzy Dean, Wilbur Voliva, Heywood Broun. But the survivors, as you will soon note, are wholly lacking in true-blue color of the authentic eccentric.

Solely as a suggested stimulus to the weak exhibitionists of the present day, I have prepared what I call an Outline of Eccentricity.

Capitalism

Cornelius Vanderbilt, the elder, kept a dish filled with salt under each leg of his bed--to scare away evil spirits, he claimed. He never owned a check book, but wrote out his checks on half-sheets of tablet paper.

Russell Sage, worth millions, rode to work daily on his five-cent elevated trains, wore eight-dollar ready-made suits, and ate apples for lunch.

Hetty Green, with her bombazine cloak, black bag and eighty million dollars, saved money on laundry bills by having only the lower half of her petticoats washed, and when her petticoats wore out, she used newspapers in their place.

Edwin Howes, the wealthy London miser, lit his pipe every morning with a one-pound British bank note.

Madame de La Bresse, of France, left her 125,000 francs to be used in purchasing clothes for snowmen.

Francesca Nortyuega, the European reformer, willed a fortune to her niece with the provision that the family goldfish be dressed in pants!

Outline of Eccentricity 77

George Francis Train ran for the Presidency of the United States, made one thousand speeches, but didn't receive a single vote. He believed he would live forever if he ate nothing but peanuts. He was buried in 1904.

Royalty

The Duke of Wellington always carried six watches on his person. "Which is why I'm always prompt," he bragged.

Frederick the Great never washed his face. He hated water. Instead, he dabbed red paint on his cheeks to make them appear healthy and clean.

Queen Catherine II, of Russia, imprisoned her hairdresser in an iron cage for three years so that there would be no gossip about the royal dandruff.

Cardinal Richelieu devoted several hours a day to leaping over furniture.

King Edward VII could not bear to hear the jingling of coins, and would allow no one in his household to carry loose change.

Literature

Hawthorne always washed his hands before reading a letter from his wife.

George Moore owned a pet python.

James Fenimore Cooper could not write unless he was chewing gum.

Dean Farrar wrote all his books while standing up.

Maurus Jokai needed violet ink.

Disraeli had to be attired in evening dress.

Mark Twain wore white suits in winter.

Lewis Carroll sported black gloves in summer. And when traveling, he demanded that every article in his trunk be wrapped separately.

Oliver Goldsmith applied for the clergy in a red suit--yes, you guessed it.

Rousseau claimed that a phantom walked continually by his side.

Alexandre Dumas could only write novels on blue paper, poetry on yellow paper, articles on rose-colored paper.

Sundry Arts

Charles Baudelaire dyed his hair a brilliant green, boasted cannibalism and lived with snakes.

Shelley folded important letters or hundred-dollar bills into toy boats and sailed them on streams.

William Blake, the poet, artist and mystic, insisted that he was a brother of Socrates and that he talked with Christ.

Niccolò Paganini, violin genius, used to play with frayed strings, hoping that one or more of them might break, so that he could display his skill on those remaining.

Whistler signed his paintings and personal correspondence with the sketch of a butterfly. And tied his forelock with a white ribbon.

Enrico Caruso would not sing in public unless he knew there were hired applauders in the audience.

Disjecta Membra

Georges Clemenceau wore slippers and gloves to bed.

Spinoza devoted hours to capturing spiders and making them fight.

Florence Nightingale carried a pet owl in her pocket.

Gerard de Nerval paraded Paris boulevards with a huge turtle at the end of a leash.... "Why not lead turtles? They do not bark. And they know the secrets of the deep!"

Outline of Eccentricity

Fritz Babel, of Munich, stayed in bed sixty years to keep from becoming ill.

George Asher, of Joplin, lived like a horse. He wore his hair to resemble a mane, had his footwear shod with horseshoes, and thrived on such delicacies as hay, grass and oats.

Harry Lehr handcuffed himself to Mrs. O. H. P. Belmont and then swallowed the key.

Timothy Dexter, who preceded Gertrude Stein by a century and a half, penned a book without punctuation, and on the last page supplied an assortment of commas, semicolons and periods for those who like to take their grammar straight. The sane Mr. Dexter shipped mittens to the South Seas, sent coal to Newcastle, and bought worthless stock, yet made a fortune on each. His front lawn was decorated with statues of Washington, Moses, and himself.

Baron Harden-Hickey composed a volume entitled, The Ethics of Suicide, wherein he suggested eighty-eight potent poisons and fifty-one novel instruments. He declared himself ruler of a barren island off the coast of South America, which brought Great Britain and Brazil to the verge of war.

The Future or Whither?

The tomorrow of eccentricity depends on a handful of unpredictable Sophists; unpredictable because this group has a tendency to capitalize materially on eccentricity, instead of living the life for its fine esthetic value alone. Among the modern white hopes are the following:

William P. Devou, of Cincinnati, worth fifteen million dollars, yet dressing like a beggar and residing in an attic.

Wilbur Voliva, of Zion City, Illinois, who contends the earth is flat like a saucer, while Columbus squirms in his grave.

Gabriele D'Annunzio, taking one hundred umbrellas to London. "There is so much moisture there," he explains.

Heywood Broun and his trousers that bag at the knees.

Herbert Bayard Swope, who sleeps in a skullcap with slickum under it to keep his hair in place.

James Montgomery Flagg, who insists he is the reincarnation of Abe Lincoln.

Dizzy Dean, who, on the hottest afternoon in baseball history, emerged from his dugout clothed in a raccoon coat, woolen blanket, and Daniel Boone cap, and then proceeded to build a bonfire.

It will be noted that temperamental movie stars and actors have been omitted from this Outline, because since they possess press agents, one cannot be sure whether the recorded eccentricity is a personal attribute or merely a publicity gag.

--Vol. 18, No. 426 (August 28, 1937), pages 8-9.

RHYTHM

by Charles Chaplin

Only the dawn moved in the stillness of that small Spanish prison yard--the dawn ushering in death, as the young Loyalist stood facing the firing squad. The preliminaries were over. The small group of officials had stepped to one side to witness the end, and now the scene had tightened into ominous silence.

Up to the last, the Rebels had hoped that a reprieve would come from headquarters, for although the condemned man was an enemy to their cause, in the past he had been a popular figure in Spain, a brilliant writer of humor, who had contributed much to the enjoyment of his fellow countrymen.

The officer in charge of the firing squad knew him personally. Before the Civil War they had been friends. Together they had been graduated from the university in

Madrid. Together they had worked for the overthrow of
the monarchy and the power of the Church. And together
they had caroused, had sat at nights around café tables, had
laughed and joked, had enjoyed evenings of metaphysical discussion. At times they had argued on the dialectics of government. Their technical differences were friendly then, but
now those differences had wrought misery and upheaval over
all Spain and had brought his friend to die by the firing
squad.

But why think of the past? Why reason? Since the
Civil War what good was reason? In the silence of the prison
yard these interrogative thoughts ran feverishly through the
officer's mind.

No. He must shut out the past. Only the future
mattered. The future? A world in which he would be deprived of many old friends.

That morning was the first time they had met since
the war. But never a word was spoken. Only a faint
smile of recognition passed between them as they prepared
for the march into the prison yard.

From the sombre dawn streaks of silver and red
peered over the prison wall and breathed a quiet requiem
in rhythm with the stillness in the yard, a rhythm pulsating
in silence like the throbbing of a heart. Out of that silence
the voice of the commanding officer resounded against the
prison walls. "Attention!"

At this command six subordinates snapped their
rifles to their sides and stiffened. The unity of their action
was followed by a pause in which the next command was to
be given.

But in that pause something happened, something that
broke the line of rhythm. The condemned man coughed and
cleared his throat. This interruption broke the concatenation
of procedure.

The officer turned, expecting the prisoner to speak,
but no words came. Turning to his men again, he was
about to proceed with the next command, but a sudden revolt
took possession of his brain, a psychic amnesia that left his
mind a blank. He stood bewildered before his men. What
was the matter? The scene in the prison yard had no

meaning. He saw only objectively--a man with his back to
the wall facing six others. And the group there on the side,
how foolish they looked, like rows of clocks that had suddenly
stopped ticking. No one moved. No one made sense. Something was wrong. It must all be a dream, and he must snap
out of it.

 Dimly his memory began to return. How long had he
been standing there? What had happened? Ah, yes! He had
issued an order. But what order came next?

 Following "attention" was the command, "present
arms," and after that, "to aim," and then "fire!" A faint
concept of this was in the back of his mind. But words to
utter it seemed far off--vague and outside of himself.

 In this dilemma he shouted incoherently, jumbled
words that had no meaning. But to his relief the men presented arms. The rhythm of their action set his brain in
rhythm, and again he shouted. Now the men took aim.

 But in the pause that followed, there came into the
prison yard hurrying footsteps the nature of which the officer
knew meant a reprieve. Instantly his mind cleared. "Stop!"
he screamed frantically at the firing squad.

 Six men stood poised with rifles. Six men were
caught in rhythm. Six men when they heard the scream to
stop--fired.

--Vol. 18, No. 445 (January
15, 1938), page 4.

EXPERIMENT IN THE DARK

by Charles Chaplin

On subjects occult, I have always kept an open mind. I believe however, that a great deal of what passes for supernatural can easily be explained. Nevertheless, there are
incidents in this story (which, incidentally, is true) that

Experiment in the Dark

transcend any rationalizing on my part, and the solution of them I must leave to the reader.

 The main incident of this narrative explains itself. The one in which I actually saw the most horrifying--but there, I'm getting ahead of my story. About a year before I built my home in Beverly Hills, I received an anonymous letter which stated that in a dream the writer had seen a newly built house with forty windows, situated on the top of a hill, which in shape was like the deck of a boat.

 In detail the writer described the house and grounds, and in the dream I was seen coming out of the house followed by a dwarf--a strange looking creature with short legs and a large torso covered with quill-like hair. As I moved about the grounds this monstrosity in mute silence, its hair rising, then settling, followed me, stopping as I stopped, moving as I moved--but keeping always a few paces behind me.

 This, the writer stated, was a warning not to build on the property I had recently purchased. "Your presence there is an intrusion, as the land is the nadir of occult forces--the sacred ground upon which thousands of years ago ancient tribes made human sacrifice."

 If, however, I was determined to build there, I should under no circumstances permit the house to be in darkness. <u>Light</u>, the writer underlined, would be my protection, and in the house it should burn continuously. The letter bore no signature, save at the end a small circle.

 Of course at the time I regarded the missive as the ravings of a crank. Nevertheless, I like to keep unusual letters, so I locked it away in my desk, and the matter was soon forgotten. And contrary to the advice of my occult friend, I eventually built my house on the so-called sacred ground.

 About six months after I had been installed in my new home, I came upon this letter again. On rereading it, I was amazed to find that the description of the house and grounds was accurate in almost every detail, and sure enough, the shape of the lawn was exactly like the deck of a boat. The "forty windows" I had not counted, but I would do so later.

That evening was the servants' night off, so I was at liberty to roam through the house alone and count windows. There were exactly forty! As I came to the last one, I felt an omnipresence, as if the room were alive and silently reproaching me.

No longer was I supercilious about the letter. I was bent, however, on verifying some of its warnings. The prospect of such an adventure thrilled me. I had been warned never to leave the house in darkness, but I had not been told what fate would befall me if I did.

So tonight I intended to find out. I would turn off every light in the house.

The time was approaching midnight. The servants usually did not return before one or two in the morning, so I had at least an hour in which to carry out my experiment.

I decided to hold the seance in the organ room, a long narrow chamber with a high Gothic ceiling and tall windows. Going through the house, I turned off all the lights, leaving the organ room until the last. Outside, the grounds were bathed in moonlight--streaks of it ran high up the lofty walls. Adjusting the curtains so that no light was visible, I finally groped my way to a large couch and sat down.

In the thick, heavy blackness I began to speculate.

Supposing a ghost did really appear. Would such a phenomenon alter my life?

In my youth I would probably have hied me to a monastery and awaited the end because then I was less interested in secular, mundane ideas. But now, on the wrong side of forty, I believed that this terrestrial existence is just as important as any other in the Hereafter. So the appearance of a ghost would make no difference.

In the midst of my reverie I was, to put it mildly, suddenly aroused by the clock striking twelve. In the dark I sat motionless, listening to the last stroke. The silence that followed was deafening. For twenty minutes I sat thus in suspense--the blackness swirling about me.

After awhile I began to realize that just to sit, wait, and concentrate was ineffectual. Speech, I decided, might be more efficacious.

Experiment in the Dark

"Is there a spirit in the house?.... If so, will you kindly materialize?"

My voice sounded hard, and I felt a little foolish. Of course nothing materialized. Perhaps I should be more supplicant, more earnest in my approach: "Oh, divine spirit, will you not give me a sign?" Histrionically, this sounded very tame.

Nevertheless, at that moment there came a loud crack. After recovering from the shock, I knew, of course, it was the house settling. It was new then and was often cracking. Still, I thought, it might be more than a coincidence.

"If that was a sign, will you answer by cracking twice?"

But there were no more cracks. In the silence that followed, only the internal whining of my stomach was audible.

The thrill of expectation by now was fast leaving me, the darkness was becoming soporific, and realizing that further talking to myself was not morally stimulating, I turned on the lights and left the room in disgust.

Turning them on in the sittingroom, I sat down at the piano hoping to dispel a rather cynical mood. Very soon I was improvising, playing strange dissonant chords. One in particular fascinated me, and I found myself repeating it until it seemed the whole house vibrated.

As I played, it occurred to me that if there were such things as ghosts, the vibration of music might be the means through which they could communicate--through which they might materialize. This was an interesting theory--music being the language of the spirits--emotions, gained from a Beethoven symphony, being abstract messages from a spirit world.

As I was thinking all this and playing these chords, I suddenly became aware of being enveloped in a white vaporous light. It seemed to be forming in front of my chest and slowly circumvesting my body, gradually tightening and paralyzing me. Instantly I leaped to my feet, and instantly the light disappeared.

Of course, after I got over the fright, I realized that the incident could be easily explained. The piano stood in the recess of a bay window. On the hill opposite was a winding road. The headlights of an automobile coming down it must have shone through the window and illuminated my chest. As I had been high-strung at the moment, my imagination had supplied the rest. Even as I was reasoning this out, the headlights of another car shone through the window.

Nevertheless, to convince myself completely, I decided to sit again at the piano and to repeat the same chords. After awhile a feeling came over me that I was not alone.

At the other end of the room was the entrance leading into the hall. From the corner of my eye, I could see something moving--the impression of something dwarfish waddling across the dimly lit hall. I turned, but only in time to see it disappear in the direction of the stairs.

But in that fleeting glimpse, just as it was described in the letter, I recognized the monster--its hair standing on end. Numbed by incredulity rather than fear, I sat and stared, then slowly got up from the piano and looked down the hall. But the creature had gone.

I tried to reason. It might have been a loose eyelash or something in the corner of my eye--such a thing could create an illusion. But what I had seen I felt sure was more than an illusion!

I could arrive at no satisfactory explanation, and deeming it unwise to dwell on the matter, as it might involve questioning my sanity, I dismissed the incident as though it had never occurred.

About ten minutes later I was upstairs in my pajamas, ready for bed. In the bathroom, I turned on the light.

Imagine my horror when I saw standing in the bathtub, peering up at me, the actual monster of the scene below. With a gasp I made a horizontal exit, slamming the door after me. Finding myself at the telephone, I yelled for the servant who by now had returned home:

"Frank! Come at once! There's a skunk in the bathroom!"

--Vol. 20, No. 476 (September 24, 1938), pages 4-5.

SHANGHAI, NOT WITHOUT GESTURES

by Louis L'Amour

She came in from the street and stood watching the auction, a slender girl with great, dark eyes and a clear, creamy complexion. It was raining outside on Kiangse Road, and her shoes were wet. From time to time she shifted uncomfortably, and glanced about. Once, her eyes met mine and I smiled, but she glanced away quickly, watching the auction.

There was always an auction somewhere, it seemed. Today it might be on Range Road, or somewhere along Route Frelupt, tomorrow it would be in Kelmscott Garden. Household effects, usually, for people were always coming or going. I knew none of them, being an outsider in Shanghai and contented with it. But I liked to come and see the things to be sold, simple things, like Soochow curtains, chests of drawers, brass-topped tea tables--the odds and ends of people's lives. I used to think up stories about them, and wonder what sort of people owned them before. It wasn't much of a pastime, but they were dark days, and it was all I could afford.

The girl interested me more. Reading or thinking stories is all right, but living is better. This girl had not come to buy, she had come in out of the wet. Probably it was cold in her rooms.

Rooms? More likely a room, and a small place, with a few simple things. There would be some worn slippers, a few neat, rather worn frocks, a Japanese silk kimono. Probably there would be a picture on the old-fashioned dresser, of a man, of course. He would be an army officer, grave and attractive.

I tried to move closer to her, for we were across the room from each other, but she noticed it and turned to go. I was persistent; when she stepped out into the rain, I was beside her.

"Wet, isn't it?" I said, hoping to hear her voice, but she hurried on, never looking at me.

"Please," I said. "I'm not getting fresh. I'm just lonely. Weren't you ever lonely?"

She walked slower then, and glanced at me quickly. Her eyes were very black, and even larger than I had believed. She smiled a little then, and she had a nice mouth. "Yes," she said, "I am often lonely."

"Would you like some coffee?" I offered, "Or tea? Or what does one drink in Shanghai?"

"Almost everything," she said, and then laughed a little. She seemed surprised at that, and looked so self-conscious I knew she was hungry. Once you have been hungry you always know about someone else. It makes you feel very different. "But I would like some coffee," she said.

We found a little place several blocks away, and sat down to look at each other. Her dark suit was a little shabby, and she seemed tired. I am sensitive to such things. There was a little accent in her voice that intrigued me, but I couldn't place it. I had heard many accents, but I was younger then, and that was the other Shanghai, the Shanghai that was before the shells of Nippon blasted Chapel into smoking ruins and destroyed the fine tempo of the life.

"You are new here?" she asked. "You don't belong here?"

"I belong nowhere," I said, "but I have just come."

"No one belongs in Shanghai. Everyone is either just going or just coming."

"You?"

She shrugged. "Like you, I belong nowhere. Shanghai more than anywhere else. I belong here because I belong nowhere, and nobody belongs in Shanghai."

"That sounds complicated," I said, liking her eyes.

"It isn't," she said simply. She moved her feet under the table and I heard them squish.

"I'm Russian," she said. "But I was born in Nanking. My father left Russia at the time of the revolution. He didn't care much about it. He first got tired of fighting, and then he got tired of talking politics. Everyone talks politics in Russia, so he came to Nanking."

"A remarkable man," I said. "I was thinking only Grand Dukes left Russia. What did he do then?"

"He drank."

"Unquestionably a remarkable man. To drink and do something is remarkable, to drink and do nothing is genius. What did he drink?"

"Madeira, then vodka, finally samshu and Hanshin."

The decline and fall of a refined palate. "And he died?"

She nodded, and I knew that was how it would be. For a man to sink from fine, old Madeira to Hanshin--after that there is nothing to do but die.

Our coffee was finished. I looked down at my cup, made a mental calculation and decided against another. "Shall we go?"

The rain had resolved itself into a fine mist, and the street lights were glowing through the fog. It would be this way all night. I saw her hesitate, and she glanced quickly at me, then held out her hand. "I'd better go."

I took her hand. "Why not come with me? It's going to be an unpleasant night." Her eyes met mine and she looked away quickly. "Why not?" I said. "It isn't much of a place, but it's warm.

"All right," she said.

We walked rapidly. It wasn't going to be a nasty night, it was already a nasty night. A taxi skidded around

the corner in a cloud of spray, and then was gone. I was
glad when we reached the door. For myself, it didn't matter.
Sometimes I walk for hours in the rain. But she wasn't
dressed very warm, and the rain was cold and miserable.
The place was warm when we got in. The boy was gone. I
called him my Number Only boy. I told him he couldn't be
a number one boy because there wasn't going to be any two,
three, or four.

    It wasn't just a room, it was a small apartment. It
was nice, in a way. Drifting men acquire the habit of fixing
up almost any place they stop to make it more homelike.
Seamen often fix things up like any old maid would do, and
perhaps for the same reason. There were a half-dozen books
lying around, and I'd picked up some woodcuts to hang on the
walls with some pictures I had. She looked at the books, and
it pleased me when she picked one up and glanced at the title.
It always makes a sucker out of a man who loves books to
see someone take an interest in them.

    When she came out of the shower she was wearing
my robe, and her eyes were very bright. I hadn't realized
she was so pretty. We sat by the fire, watching the coals.

    "Lose your job?" I said finally.

    She nodded. "Two weeks ago. My rent was up last
week. This morning they said not to come back unless I
could pay."

    "That's tough. What's your line?"

    "Anything. I'm a secretary, usually. Sometimes I
sell. But anything around an office. I worked for Moran &
Company, in Tientsin. Then here, for a transport firm.
But there has been so little business. I don't know what I'm
going to do."

    Outside was China. Outside was Shanghai. Three
million people: English, French, Dutch, American, Sikh,
German, Russian, Portuguese, Spanish, Dane, Norwegian,
Japanese, Hebrew, Greek, Armenian, Malay, and, always
and forever, the Chinese. Outside was the Whangpoo, a
dark river flowing out of China, out of old China into new
China, and down to the sea. Outside were rivers of men
flowing back and forth along the dark streets, men buying
and selling, men fighting and gambling, men loving and dying.

Three million men and women of all colors and kinds, opening countless doors, eating the food of many countries, speaking a hundred languages, praying to many gods.

I listened to her voice, and remembered the shuffle of the feet in the noontime streets. There was nothing I could do. It is bad for a man to be broke, but so much worse for a woman. Especially such a girl as this. Maybe I was a fool, but I, too, have been hungry. Tomorrow, if I wished, there was a ship. I could go to Batavia, to Bombay, to Liverpool, or New York. While she....

"You wouldn't have come with me if there had been any other place to go, would you?"

She didn't look up, but after awhile, she whispered, "No." A lock of her dark hair had fallen against my robe. It looked so very black against the soft white of her throat. "But I am grateful. What could I have done?"

Well what? I had a feeling I was going to make a fool of myself. Americans are too sentimental, and every cynic is a sentimentalist under the skin. I knew enough about women to be a skeptic, but had been hungry enough to be human.

"Listen," I said, "this isn't quite the sporting thing, is it? To have you come here because you were cold and because I bought you a cup of coffee? Or maybe because of breakfast in the morning? I don't like the sound of it. Well, hell, I'm going to sleep on the daybed here, you can sleep in the other room. If you change your mind ...well...."

After the door closed I stood looking at it. If she hadn't been so damned lovely it would have been easier to do the gallant thing. And probably right now she was thinking what a sap I was. Well, she wouldn't be the only one thinking that.

I was going to be sorry for this in the morning.

> --Vol. 21, No. 508 (May 13, 1939), pages 6-7.

LITTLE ORSON ANNIE

by Gene Lockhart

Little Orson Annie's come to our town to play,
An' josh the motion pictures up, an' skeer the stars away,
An' shoo the laughtons off the lot, an' build the sets an' sweep,
An' take the film, an' write the talk, an' earn her board-an'-keep;
An' all us other acters, when our pitchur work is done,
We set around the Derby bar an' has the mostest fun,
A-list'nin' to the me-tales 'at Annie spreads about,
An' the Gobble-welles 'at gits you
    Ef you
        Don't
            Watch
                Out!

Onc't there wuz a acter man tried to add a line--
An' when he played a scene in bed and hoped to shine,
His agent heerd him holler, his manager heerd him bawl,
An' when they turn't the kivvers down, he wuzn't there at all!
An' they seeked him in his dressing-room, and told it to the press,
An' seeked him in the Masquers Club, an' ever'wheres, I guess,
But all they ever found was this, his pants, an' script, an' clout!--
An' the Gobble-welles'll git you
    Ef you
        Don't
            Watch
                Out!

An' one time a ingenue 'ud allus laugh an' grin,
An' giggle at the Orsonwoof, and at his discipline;
An' onc't when they wuz in a scene, an' "company" wuz there,
She mocked him, an' she shocked him, an' said she didn't care!
An' thist as she kicked up her heels an' turn't to run an' hide,

They wuz a great big Brown Beard a-stridin' by her side,
An' it <u>snatched</u> her from the pitchur 'fore she knowed what
   she's about!
An' the Gobble-welles'll git you
    Ef you
      Don't
        Watch
          Out!

An' little Orson Annie says, when the talk is blue,
An' the camera sputters, an' the sound goes whoo!
An' you hear the scrip' girl quake, an' the crew looks gray,
An' the casting-office man has faint-ed away--
You better mind yer cues an' yer director fond an' dear,
An' churish him 'at hired you, an' 'bedient appear,
An' he'p the pore old Fuddledy Beard 'at rushes all about,
Er the Gobble-welles'll git <u>you</u>
    Ef you
      Don't
        Watch
          Out!

                          --Vol. 23, No. 539 (January
                          27, 1940), page 4.

SHOW ME THE WAY TO GO HOME

by Louis L'Amour

It was the night the orchestra played "Show Me the Way to Go Home," the night the fleet sailed for Panama. The slow drizzle of rain had stopped, and there was nothing but the play of searchlights across the clouds, the mutter of the motors from the shore boats, and the spatter of grease where the man was frying hamburgers on the Fifth Street landing. I was standing there with a couple of Greek fishermen and a taxi driver, watching the gobs say good-bye to their wives and sweethearts.

    There was something about the smell of rain, the sailors saying good-bye, and the creak of rigging that sort of got to you. I'd been on the beach for a month then.

A girl came down to the landing and leaned on the rail watching the shore boats. One of the gobs waved at her, and she waved back, but didn't smile. You could see that they didn't know each other; it was just one of those things.

She was alone. Every other girl was with somebody, but not her. She was wearing a neat, tailored suit that was a little worn, but she had nice legs and large, expressive eyes. When the last of the shore boats was leaving she was still standing there. Maybe it wasn't my move, but I was lonely, and when you're on the beach you don't meet many girls. So I walked over and leaned on the rail beside her.

"Saying good-bye to your boy friend?" I asked, though I knew she wasn't.

"I said good-bye to him a long time ago."

"He didn't come back?"

"Do they ever?"

"Sometimes they want to and can't. Sometimes things don't break right."

"I wonder."

"And sometimes they do come back and things aren't like they were, and sometimes they don't come back because they are afraid they won't be the same, and they don't want to spoil what they remember."

"Then why go?"

"Somebody has to. Men have always gone to sea, and girls have waited for them."

"I'm not waiting for anybody."

"Sure you are. We all are. From the very beginning we wait for somebody, watch for them long before we know who they are. Sometimes we find the one we wait for, sometimes we don't. Sometimes the one we wait for comes along and we don't know it until too late. Sometimes they ask too much and we are afraid to take a chance, and they slip away."

Show Me the Way to Go Home

"I wouldn't wait for anyone. Especially him. I wouldn't want him now."

"Of course not. If you saw him now you'd wonder why you ever wanted him. You aren't waiting for him, though--you're waiting for what he represented. You knew a sailor once. Girls should never know men who have the sea in their blood."

"They always go away."

"Sure, and that's the way it should be. All the sorrow and tragedy in life come from trying to make things last too long."

"You're a cynic."

"All sentimentalists are cynics, and all Americans are sentimentalists. It's the Stephen Foster influence. Or too many showings of Over the Hill to the Poorhouse and East Lynne. But I like it that way."

"Do people really talk like this?"

"Only when they need coffee. Or maybe the first time a girl and a man meet. Or maybe this talk is a result of the saying good-bye influence. It's the same thing that makes women cry at the weddings of perfect strangers."

"You're a funny person." She turned to look at me.

"I boast of it. But how about that coffee? We shouldn't stand here much longer. People who lean on railings over water at night are either in love or contemplating suicide."

We started up the street. This was the sort of thing that made life interesting--meeting people. Especially attractive blondes at midnight.

Over the coffee she looked at me. "A girl who falls in love with a sailor is crazy."

"Not at all. A sailor always goes away, and then she doesn't have time to be disillusioned. Years later she can make her husband's life miserable telling him what a wonderful man so-and-so was. The chances are he was a fourteen-carat sap. Only he left before the new wore off."

"Is that what you do?"

"Very rarely. I know all the rules for handling women. The trouble is that at the psychological moment I forget to use them. It's depressing."

"It's getting late. I'm going to have to go home."

"Not alone, I hope."

She looked at me again, very coolly. "You don't think I'm the sort of girl you can just pick up, do you?"

"Of course not," I chuckled. "But I wished on a star out there. You know that old gag."

She laughed. "I think you're a fool."

"That cinches it. Women always fall in love with fools. I remember some of the fellows girls loved that I wanted."

"You think it is so easy to fall in love as that?"

"It must be. Some people fall in love with no visible reason, either material, moral, or maternal. Anyway, why should it be so complicated?"

"Were you ever in love?"

"I think so. I'm not exactly sure. She was a wonderful cook, and if the way to a man's heart is through his stomach this was a case of love at first bite."

"Do you ever take anything seriously?"

"I'm taking you seriously. But why not have a little fun with it? There's only one thing wrong with life; people don't love enough, they don't laugh enough--and they are too damned conventional. Even their love affairs are supposed to run true to form. But this is spontaneous. You walk down where the sailors are saying good-bye to their sweethearts because you said good-bye to one once. It has been raining a little, and there is a sort of melancholy tenderness in the air. You are remembering the past, not because of him, because his face and personality have faded, but because of the romance of saying good-bye, the smell of strange odors from foreign ports, the thought the ocean always brings to people--romance, color, distance. A sort of vague sadness that is almost a happiness. And then, accompanied by the sound of distant music and the perfume of frying onions, I come into your life!"

She laughed again. "That sounds like a line."

"It is. Don't you see? When you went down to the landing tonight you were looking for me. You didn't know who I was, but you wanted something, someone. Well, here I am. The nice part of it is, I was looking for you."

"You make it sound very nice."

"Why not? A man who couldn't make it sound nice while looking at you would be too dull to live. Now finish your coffee and we'll go home."

"Now listen, I...."

"I know. Don't say it. But I'll just take you to the door, kiss you very nicely, and close it."

There had been another shower, and the streets were damp. A fog was rolling from the ocean, the silent mist creeping in around the corners of the buildings, encircling the ships to the peaks of their masts. It was a lonely, silent world where the street lights floated in ghostly radiance.

"You were wondering why men went to sea. Can't you imagine entering a strange, far-eastern port on such a night as this? The lights of an unknown city--strange odors, mysterious sounds, the accents of a strange tongue? It's the charm of the strange and the different, of something new. Yet there's the feeling around you of something very old. Maybe that's why men go to sea."

"Maybe it is, but I'd never fall in love with another sailor."

"I don't blame you."

We had reached the door. She put her key in the lock, and we stepped in. It was very late, and very quiet. I took her in my arms, kissed her goodnight, and closed the door.

"I thought you said you were going to say goodnight, and then go?" she protested.

"I said I was going to kiss you goodnight, and then close the door. I didn't say on which side of it I'd be."

"Well...."

The hell of it was my ship was sailing in the morning.

--Vol. 25, No. 581 (January 4, 1941), pages 6-7.

TO MAKE A LONG STORY MUCH SHORTER

by Ray Bradbury

The ocean was angry. It was lifting up huge waves like wet fists and smacking them down and making sloppy noises and being insufferably nasty about the whole thing. The lightning came down on cue and the thunder belched and the ship on which our hero and heroine were traveling was being pummeled this way and that until they were so sick they didn't know the way to the bathroom.

After about twenty-four hours of this the ship yielded up the ghost. It gave off a tremendous squealing and grating and rivets flew apart and the ship began to sink.

Of course everybody screamed and scampered for the lifeboats and the chaos was horrid.

Our hero and heroine got in a lifeboat with twenty other guys and somehow they got away from the ship just in time to see the old iron crate stick its shaking fanny up in the rain and go gurgling down into Davy Jones' parlor.

So the ship was gone and a thousand or more people were drowning right and left and maybe twelve lifeboats were bobbling about on the wave breasts and everybody was praying and crying and it was quite a mess.

To Make a Long Story Much Shorter

But there were complications. In the boat where our hero and heroine were located the people soon found out that there was too much weight and that if someone didn't volunteer to jump overboard there would be a major catastrophe for all of them.

So the hero got up in the prow of the lifeboat and shouted against the storm:

"We'll sink in a few minutes unless some of you get out! The boat is loaded too full! Who will volunteer to take a chance on swimming for land?"

(Note: Nearest land was two thousand miles away.)

A large silence followed in the wake of our hero's speech. A few people grumbled and some of them shifted about uneasily.

The rain rushed down in a welter of sound and luminating lightning.

"I'm asking for volunteers!" cried our hero. "This is a crucial moment. Someone must leave the boat!"

The heroine crouched at his feet, shivering.

"Do I hear any volunteers?" cried the hero.

No volunteers.

Finally, a little timid man in the far end of the boat stood up and pointed straight at our hero and bellowed:

"Why don't you jump over? Why don't you?"

Our hero turned to see who the little man was pointing at, and since there was no one behind him, he realized that the little man had him on the spot.

He pretended that he did not hear the little man.

"Well?" He surveyed the group with hard, gray eyes. "What are we waiting for? Look at these little children and these women! We must save them! Who'll be the first?"

"You be first!" insisted the little man.

"You, old man," demanded the hero, "why don't you dive overboard and save the lives of all these people?"

"I'm an old man and I want to live some more," replied the old man. "I've got a right to live. I got brains."

This stumped the hero.

"There must be <u>someone</u> here who will sacrifice," he said.

"Yes." It was the little timid man in the far end of the boat again, damn him. "Why don't you? Why is it always the old men and the old women who must sacrifice? None of us wish to die. Why not toss over a few children? This is a wicked world anyway and they'll be better off dead. Or better still, and I hate to repeat myself, why don't you go?"

"Yes, why don't you?" echoed several others, belligerently.

The whole boat joined in enthusiastically then. It had been decided, by judge and jury, quickly, that the hero would jump overboard.

The heroine arose swiftly, and put her arms about the hero.

"If he goes," she declared triumphantly, I'll go with him."

"But I'm not going!" said the hero.

"Oh yes you are," screamed the little man. "Toss them both over."

And the nearest fellows to the hero and heroine scrambled forward, clutched them and threw them overboard.

And the rain rained and the thunder thundered.

"Now," said the little man, "we must decide on one more person. The boat is still too heavy. One more person. Who shall it be?"

But before he could say much more everybody started arguing. They argued and argued.

And before long the whole lifeboat turned over and sank, ending the argument.

Ending the story.

> --Vol. 26, No. 606 (July 5, 1941), page 25.

THE MIKADO -- 1942

by Gene Lockhart

(Offstage: a sudden explosion of bombs, followed by sound of dive bombers.)

(Onstage: Japanese Nobles discovered standing and sitting in attitudes of listening.)

Chorus of Nobles

If you want to know who we are,
    We are gentlemen of Japan;
We dickered with F. D. R.,
    To cover our clever plan;
A Nipponese bluff and feint,
    With platitudes queer and quaint,
You're wrong if you think it ain't--
    Oh!

If you know we are worked by strings
    Like a Nazi marionette,
You will understand these things;
    It is Axis etiquette.
We thought when we jumped the gong,
    We'd keep it up all year long;
It seems we are somehow wrong--
    Ouch!

TWO LITTLE MEN

<u>Duet</u>

Two little men, two Japs are we,
   Sly as a crafty Jap can be,
Filled to the brim with ghoulish glee,
   Two little Japs are we.

<u>Kurusu</u>

Sudden attacks are a source of fun.
     (Chuckle.)

<u>Nomura</u>

Nobody's safe, for we care for none!
     (Chuckle.)

<u>Kurusu</u>

War is a joke that's just begun!
     (Chuckle.)

<u>Both</u>

Two little Japs are we!
     (Sucking of breath.)

<u>Both</u>

Two little men who, slick and wary,
   Planned a delay quite temporary,
Aiding our party military,
   Two little Saps--
     Are We!

    (Enter Mikado, with retinue of totalitarian dignitaries.)

<u>Ensemble</u>

Iyma Jappa, Iyma sappa,
   To jipp Uncley Sam,
Double talkee, plankee walkee,
   Wotanassyam!

The Mikado -- 1942

"MY OBJECT ALL SUBLIME"

(<u>The Mikado</u>)

A more insane Mikado never
    Did in Japan exist,
To nobody second,
    I'm certainly reckoned
A mad philanthropist,
    It is my very insane endeavor
To make, to some extent,
    Each yellow belly
A mass of jelly
    For Nazi merriment.

<u>Refrain</u>

My object all sublime
    I shall achieve in time,
To shift the punishment for the crime,
    The punishment for the crime,
And make each warrior bent,
    Unwillingly represent
Totalitarian merriment,
    ... itarian merriment.

<u>Ensemble of Totalitarians</u>

His object all sublime, (etc).

THE BOMBERS THAT BOOM
IN THE SPRING

Duet (<u>Ribbentrop and Mikado</u>)

Your bombers that boom in the spring,
    Tra la,
Breathe promise of victories fine,
As we slowly retreat in the cold,
    Tra la,
We welcome the hope that they hold,
    Tra la,
For all of der Fuehrer's schwein--
    For all of der Fuehrer's schwein;
And that's what I mean when I say
    that no thing

Is welcome as bombers that boom in
    the Spring;
        Tra la la la la la, etc.

Mikado

My bombers that boom in the spring,
    Alas,
Have nothing to do with the case.
I've got to take under my wing,
    Alas,
A totalitarian thing,
    Alas,
A caricature of a race,
A caricature of a race;
    And that's what I mean when I say,
        or I sing,
We won't have a bomber to boom in
    the Spring,
        Tra la la la la, tra la la la la, etc.

(Exeunt Japs and Nazis.)

DIPLOMAT'S SONG

At a desk in Nippon a little jap-wit,
    Sang, "Lano, delano, delano!"
And I said to him, "Kurusu, why do
    you sit,
    Singing, 'Lano, delano, delano'?
Is it weakness of frankness, Kurusu?"
    I cried,
    "Or a rather tough Yank that you
        thought you could ride?"
With a shake of his poor worried head
    he replied,
    "Oh, Lano, delano, delano!"

He closed up his brief case with papers
    and all,
    Singing, "Lano, delano, delano!"
And a cold perspiration broke out on
    his poll,
    "Oh, Lano, delano, delano!"
He sobbed and he sighed, and a gurgle

The Mikado -- 1942

    he gave,
Then he plunged himself into a billowy wave,
And an echo arose from the diplomat's grave--
"Oh, Lano, delano, delano!"

FINALE

The threatened cloud will pass
    away,
As brightly shines another day,
The Rising Sun, it rose too soon,
    But we have years of afternoon!

Then let the Yanks, with joy advance,
    With laughing pranks, and merry
    dance,
With joyous shout and flags unfurled,
    Inaugurate a brave new World,
Inaugurate a brave ... New ...
    World!
    Then let the Yanks, etc., etc.

--Vol. 27, No. 619 (January 3, 1942), page 22.

EPILOGUE BY AN OLD PUPIL

by José Rodriguez

The essence of Rob Wagner's life was to reconcile a refractory world to the laws and ways of beauty.

    He used the word "beauty" in a very comprehensive sense. It was not to him a concept restricted to the formal arts. It was, indeed, the substance and the motive that distinguishes truth from falsity. So it followed logically that as artist, writer and teacher, he should extend the meaning of "beautiful" to embrace justice and health, laughter and friendship, and all the things toward which we instinctively turn our hopes.

To any artist, to any philosopher--and Rob Wagner was both--the idea of finality was at once hateful and ridiculous. The eternal curve of movement, whether in the atomic minuteness of a diamond's structure, the incomprehensible majesty of the stars, the lithe animality of an athlete or the flowing harmony of a cathedral, or an engine, or a wave, was to him the one and the supreme experience.

He was himself a creature of movement. His mind never rested; his glance was full of vivacity; physical inactivity pained him. Only in the last years did he learn to appreciate and relish very short periods of complete rest. He did this somewhat like the Stoics, who went without food for a long time in order to taste the exquisite flavor of a dry crust. He always went back to his work--for his thought never ceased--with a boyish whoop of regained delight.

His contempt for the idea of finality and his love of movement manifested itself in some ways that will always be cherished when we recall those things that were uniquely Wagneresque. He avoided good-byes that went beyond a quick smile, the touch of hands and a gay word. Whenever he left a party he did so almost surreptitiously. I knew why, and once twitted him about it. It was because he disliked the lame and fatigued end of happy chatter, the turning out of lights, the reassertion of a prosy world over a fugitive but charming time of play.

Rob Wagner had two very precious gifts: an insatiable curiosity and a passion for expression. They led him naturally to many fields of work. He was trained as an engineer, he became a remarkable technician in painting, he investigated everything that came under his eye or within his hearing. And afterward he bent all his energy to explanation, to make clear the body and the meaning and the consequence of what he had examined and understood.

I prefer, therefore, to regard Rob Wagner as primarily a teacher, an inspired teacher, the most distinguished and noble title a man can earn. He taught by both precept and stimulation. First he appealed, in a way that was powerfully subtle because it was unpremeditated, to our generosity, to that spiritual quality that makes it natural and desirable to love the work at hand. Then he skillfully demonstrated the mechanics. And always, in his witty and robust manner, he impressed upon us that there was a definite and even

Epilogue by an Old Pupil

inexorable affinity between the work in our hands and our share in the shaping of the world that should use that work.

If this was true in the schoolroom, it was underlined in the editorial office. Those of us who went to school under Rob Wagner knew it already; but many who were associated with him, many who were his professional superiors only in the sense that they employed his talents, received the same training without being aware of it.

I doubt if two men have ever held a long friendship who did not sometime pause to exchange reflections on the secrets of death and immortality. Particularly, when those two men stood--as Rob and I did--in the relation of intellectual father and son. He told me many times that there was hardly room in the traditional concept of immortality for such a poor thing as personal egoism; that he did not want a disembodied Rob Wagner wandering about the cosmos with nothing to do. But that whatever claim he--or any other man--might have to immortality, lay in the work he left behind him, or in the work of those minds that he had touched and made aware.

I remember that conversation very well. It was on a warm summer day, very much like this one. I had been helping him to fell a eucalyptus tree. I can still see the broken sunlight lighting up that silver thatch of his, and his vivid, penetrating blue eyes looking up, in a rare moment of solemnity, toward the infinitely pure and imperturbable blue of the sky.

I said to myself then, while Rob went on with his chopping, "This is the first time I have realized, or noticed, the heritage of mortality that is also Rob Wagner's, as it is mine and everybody else's." And, as young men very seldom do, I also saw clearly my responsibility, and that of the better others, who had followed and loved and known Rob Wagner.

Rob has left us, I now see in reviewing the episodes of his physical presence among us, very much as he would have wished to leave us. But in reviewing the powder-train of ideas and hopes and attitudes that he left us to follow, I can also affirm that indeed he has not disappeared at all. No one more than Rob had a right to expect that immortality that keeps eternally green in loving minds and blossoms in loving hearts.

Let these poor words attest to this, Rob, that in farewell to you I have spoken truthfully and no more--as you would have ordered me to do before your friends, and in behalf of them all.

--Vol. 27, No. 634 (August 1, 1942), page 5.

GIVE US MORE BOMBS OVER BERLIN

by Charles Chaplin

On the battlefields of Russia, democracy will live or die. The fate of the Allied Nations is in the hands of the Communists. If Russia is defeated, the Asiatic continent--the largest and richest on this globe--would be under the domination of the Nazis. With practically the whole Orient in the hands of the Japanese, the Nazis will then have access to nearly all the vital war materials of the world. What chance would we have then of defeating Hitler?

With the difficulty of transportation, the problem of our communication lines thousands of miles away--the problem of steel, oil and rubber--and Hitler's strategy of divide and conquer, we would be in a desperate position if Russia should be defeated.

Some people say it would prolong the war ten or twenty years. In my estimation, this is putting it optimistically. Under such conditions--and against such a formidable enemy-- the future would be very uncertain.

The Russians are in desperate need of help. They are pleading for a second front. In the Allied Nations there is a difference of opinion as to whether a second front is possible now. We hear that the Allies haven't sufficient supplies to support a second front. Then again we hear they have. We also hear that they don't want to risk a second front at this time in case of possible defeat; that they don't want to take a chance until they are sure and ready.

But can we afford to wait until we are sure and ready? Can we afford to play safe? There is no safe strategy in war. At this moment the Germans are thirty-five miles from the Caucasus. If the Caucasus is lost, ninety-five per cent of the Russian oil is lost.

When tens of thousands are dying and millions are about to die, we must speak honestly what's on our minds. The people are asking themselves questions. We hear of great expeditionary forces landing in Ireland; ninety-five per cent of our convoys successfully arriving in Europe; two million Englishmen--fully equipped--raring to go. What are we waiting for when the situation is so desperate in Russia?

Note, Official Washington and Official London: These are not questions to create dissension. We ask them in order to dispel confusion and to engender confidence and unity for eventual victory. And whatever the answer is, we can take it.

Russia is fighting with her back against the wall. That wall is the Allies strongest defense. We defended Libya--and lost. We defended Crete--and lost. But we cannot afford to lose Russia, for that is the aggressive front line of democracy. When our world--our life--our civilization are crumbling about our feet--we've got to take a chance and save them.

If the Russians lose the Caucasus, it will be the greatest disaster to the Allied cause. Then watch out for the appeasers, for they'll come out of their holes. They will want to make peace with the victorious Hitler. They will say, "It is useless to sacrifice any more American lives-- we can make 'a good deal' with Hitler."

Watch out for this Nazi snare. These nazi wolves will change into sheep's clothing. They will make peace very attractive to us--and then before we are aware of it, we will have succumbed to the Nazi ideology. Then we shall be enslaved. They will take away our liberty, control our minds, change our language and dominate our lives. The world will be ruled by the Gestapo. They will rule us from the air. Yes--that's the power of the future.

With the power of the skies in Nazi hands, all opposition to the Nazi order will be bombed and blasted out of existence. Human progress will be lost. There will be no minority rights, no workers' rights, no citizens' rights. All that will be blasted, too. Once we listen to the appeasers and make peace with a victorious Hitler, his brutal order will control the earth.

Watch out, you guardians of democracy, you lovers of liberty and free speech! Never let them police us from the air. Watch out for the appeasers who always crop up after a disaster. But if we are on the watch, and if we keep up our morale, we have nothing to fear. Remember morale saved England. And if we keep our morale, victory is assured.

Hitler has taken many chances. His biggest one is the Russian campaign. God help him if he's not able to break through the Caucasus this summer. God help him if he has to go through another Winter around Moscow. His chance is a precarious one, but he's taken it. If Hitler can take chances why can't we?

Give us action. Give us more bombs over Berlin. Give us those Glenn Martin sea-planes to help our transport problem. Above all, give us a second front--now!

Let us aim for victory in the Spring. *You* in the factories, *you* in the fields, *you* in uniforms, *you* citizens of the democracies, *you* in all the occupied countries of the world, let us work and fight towards that end. *You*, official Washington, and *you*, official London, let us make this our aim-- victory in the Spring.

If we hold this thought, work with this thought, live with this thought, it will generate a spirit that will increase our energy and quicken our drive.

Let us strive for the impossible. Remember--the great achievements throughout the history of mankind have been the conquest of what seemed the impossible.

--Vol. 27, No. 634 (August 1, 1942), page 8.

I LIKE TO REMEMBER

by Eddie Cantor

When people start reminiscing, they're either sentimental or growing old. I happen to be very sentimental.

There are certain things I like to remember--like that afternoon during the last war, when, with Van & Schenck, the greatest of all harmony teams, I went to a hospital in Boston to entertain some wounded soldiers. Van and Schenck made the rounds, ward after ward. At one point, a doctor warned them, "Don't go in there, boys. That's the 'flu' ward." I like to remember Gus Van's answer: "Listen, Doc, Joe Schenck and I used to be conductor and motorman on a Brooklyn trolley. Do you think any 'flu' germ would frighten us?"

The night of December 3, 1923, in Detroit, the opening of Kid Boots. After the performance, the great Ziegfeld came backstage. He told the company: "We've got a smash hit. Please don't wire, phone or write to anybody--in New York about it. They'll expect too much--promise?" And that night, in Ziegfeld's suite at the Statler Hotel, I watched him send telegrams to every dramatic critic and editor in New York, and every ticket-broker and friend. All the profit of Kid Boots for that week went to Western Union.

Will Rogers Telling President Woodrow Wilson, "Mr. President, Congress'll be asking you how you can get an army ready so fast. You tell 'em that when you teach an army to go one way, you can do it in half the time." Yes sir, I like to remember Will Rogers,--philosopher, humorist, prophet--and grand human being.

George Jessel and this writer staying up all night at the Edison Hotel in New York to "frame" a vaudeville show, which opened the next day at the Palace Theater, and broke a record by staying there for nine weeks. Jessel's ad libbing at the opening matinee ... for instance: "Cantor is the only guy I know who stops at Albuquerque and sells blankets to the Indians!"

That morning when the youngster Deanna Durbin was going to audition for me. On the way to the studio, she took my hand and said, "I hope you're not nervous!" I had a feeling that moment, and it was borne out a few minutes later, that the gal had to be a star.

When I got Maurice Evans to sing a hot version of "Daddy" on my radio program, and his remark, when I met him a week later, "Cantor, you've ruined my career. I remember when I walked down the street and people would say, 'There goes Maurice Evans, the Shakespearian actor,' Now they point at me and say, 'Here comes Hot-Lips Maury!'"

The song "Makin' Whoopee," with the very gorgeous Gladys Glad, Hazel Forbes, Myrna Darby, Jean Ackerman and the Howard Twins. Never was a comedian surrounded by so much pulchritude.

I like to remember the night we introduced a song called "We're Having a Baby" in Banjo Eyes. I forgot my lyrics, and the other half of the duet, June Clyde, pretending to kiss me, whispered every word into my ear.

Those eighteen days in England--July, 1938--when the British people gave this beggar $560,000 to help remove children from Hitler's Hell. Especially that midnight performance at the Kilburn Theater in London, when I had the great joy of introducing every big star in England, and the thrill, at 3:30 a.m., of seeing Gracie Fields discard the microphone and sing and sing and sing. The receipts for that show were $45,000. It's a night I like to remember!

Sidney Franklin, really fighting a ferocious bull on the back lot at the United Artists Studios in Hollywood. The late Douglas Fairbanks, Charlie Chaplin and myself watching Franklin in the most daring exhibition I've ever seen. The next afternoon Sidney and I were going to lunch. It took him three minutes to make up his mind to cross the intersection of Hollywood and Vine. I asked him what was the matter. And he told me, "The traffic in this town--it scares the daylights out of me!"

The Sunday night on that coffee program, when a girl came on and stole the show. Her partner, who helped write the material, thanked me for giving her the opportunity. The following week they decided to try radio on their own. They're still at it--Burns and Allen.

The time Frank Loesser dropped in at the house to play a song he had written. "This may never catch on," he said, "but you should sing it--it would be good for you." If Loesser is reading this, I want to surprise him: the song, "Praise the Lord and Pass the Ammunition," has caught on.

I like to remember the soldiers, sailors and marines at the various camps, Naval and Marine bases, before whom I've appeared. Their laughter and applause. You'd think we entertainers were really doing something for them!

I like to remember Al Jolson, Joe E. Brown and Bob Hope winging thousands of miles and, by their personalities and talent, lifting the spirits of Uncle Sam's nephews for a little while.

I like to remember Abbott and Costello, Jack Benny, Dorothy Lamour, Marlene Dietrich, Dinah Shore, Bing Crosby, Kay Kyser, Edgar Bergen and hundreds of other performers who became super-salesmen, selling hundreds of millions of dollars' worth of bonds for their Government.

Carole Lombard, who gave her life for her country ...

I like America to remember!

--Vol. 29, No. 653 (May 1, 1943), page 8.

COMICS AND THE WAR

by Eddie Cantor

Maybe it is going a little too far to say that an army travels on its belly laughs. You can't stop a Stuka with a well-placed gag. A Panzer Division has no ribs that can be tickled. But, given an equal weight in armaments, pin your faith on the nation that can pack punch in its lines as well as its battles!

Have you ever seen pictures of a laughing Nazi, Fascist or Nippon? I haven't. The Nazi "supermen," no matter which way they are retreating, are always pictured as grim, forbidding and humorless. Just a lot of sour pusses! They are all imitation hams, patterned after the prize "porkers" of them all--Hitler and his end-men, Mussolini and Hirohito. That trio is awful funny, only they don't realize it! If there weren't a thousand other reasons, their routines alone ought to earn them history's hook.[1]

On the other hand, the United Nations, fighting for the right to laugh and let laugh--all four freedoms rolled into one--offer innumerable instances of a real appreciation of laughter. Winston Churchill, in his last two or three speeches in Washington and Canada, has become the envy of every comic within earshot. Many a right arm would gladly have been offered to get the guffaws Mr. Churchill got! Our Own F.D.R., personifying the humanity of America in his heartwarming smile, has provided his countrymen with many an inspiring chuckle. Newsmen in Washington flock to the Presidential press conferences not only for news but for laughs. Even the gallant Russians are showing healthy humor as they blitz the Fritz. They're hitting with everything they've got, including some witty poster appeals to their people, according to recent photographs from abroad.

Fellows, like myself, however, who've dedicated themselves through peace and war to the funnier sides of life, cannot abdicate just because we are not directing military operations against the enemy. We have a vital function to perform on the home front.

You can't laugh a bomb out of the sky, but you can drag many a penny hidden under mattresses and in cups in the cupboards by a line like Fibber McGee's: "Buy a Bond and Slap a Jap across the Pond." A gag can be as effective as a hundred billboards or five hundred newspaper stories.

In his report on the state of the nation, the President said that every one of us has accepted the challenge of the enemy in both an individual and joint manner. Even though we comics appear to be taking the situation lightly, we are not! We'll bring up the sights on our own line of production. True, we cannot build tanks, planes and ships, but if hitting the funnybone can help the men who do, you can count on the

---
1. Benito just got it.

Comics and the War

Fibber McGees and Mollys, the Bob Hopes, Red Skeltons, Jack Bennys, Edgar Bergen-Charlie McCarthys, the Groucho Marxes, Fred Allens, Abbott and Costellos; the Fannie Brices and Burns and Allens.

All of them are ready to help twist the boche's tail. The job is no laughable one, but when it's over, we'll have reason to be joyful about it. All of us are ready to pitch all along the line.

This being war, you hear people everywhere talking about the "escapist" movie and show--particularly, where they apply to comics. Laughter is supposed to be a method of getting away from it all. Maybe it is. Maybe people today want to forget about themselves and the bitter realities of the headlines. I don't think, however, that comedy is just a sugar-coated bromide.

A laugh a day will keep the dastards[2] away. We all want to laugh--the minute we stop wanting to, we'll really be on the skids. Laughter is an oxygen tank for free-breathing democracy. The countries that do not permit the absolute freedom of laughter will sink first. It takes the courage of a laugh to face adversity and see it through.

For my fellow creators of laughter, for the men and women who aim their barbs at America's risibilities, I want to enlist all the way towards winning the war. The barrage of laughs that lifts the morale of our men, women and children is an important reserve to the barrage of bombs that are hurled forth to meet the enemy. High spirits are one of this country's first priorities.

Yes, it's war. Leave it to the comedians to help rout General Calamity and Major Catastrophe.

--Vol. 29, No. 661 (August 28, 1943), page 7.

---

2. No typographical error. Script is a family magazine.

EXAMPLE

by Jessamyn West

I passed an old man
walking in the rain.
"God bless old men
And take away their pain."

I kept my eyes shut
while I was praying
But I said, "God, note
What I've been saying."

"Note the tender kindness
To a stranger done.
And remember our relation
Is a closer one."

     --Vol. 29, No. 663 (September
     25, 1943), page 5.

THROUGH A GLASS DARKLY

by Jessamyn West

Between the world and me
I only intervene.
If I could disappear
pure world could then be seen.

But when I try to vanish
the world goes, too.
My deep opacity is what
I must see through.

     --Vol. 29, No. 663 (September
     25, 1943), page 5.

A SALUTE TO RUSSIA

by Charlie Chaplin

Twenty-six years ago a brave new world was born that gave hope and inspiration to the common man. That world was Soviet Russia, imbued with a dream that would give its people, no matter what race or color, their natural rights to equal liberty, equal justice, and equal opportunity in the pursuit of food and shelter and the life beautiful. And in spite of the ravages of wars, that dream has become a reality, and grows more glorious year by year. Now that the agony of birth is at an end, may the beauty of its growth endure forever.

--Vol. 29, No. 667 (November 20, 1943), page 25.

THE COMMON MAN

by Ben Hecht

> This skit, with lyrics by E. Y. Harburg and music by Burton Lane, was enacted at a mass meeting sponsored by the Citizens Committee at the Shrine Auditorium for Vice-President Wallace.

A light, stage left, points up the ticket seller's booth. The music plays circus music as the people wander on stage, crowding around the booth.

BALLOT MAN:
    Here y'are, folks! Come up and get your ballots. Can't vote without a ballot! Step up, here's your ballot for the World of Tomorrow ... the only genuine ticket to Democracy.

GIRL:
What do you have to be to get a ballot?

BALLOT MAN:
You gotta be twenty-one--and you gotta be people.

GIRL:
People?

BALLOT MAN:
Yes, people! Haven't you ever heard of people? Step up--meet the people.

Song "Meet the People." Curtain opens.

BALLOT MAN:
Folks, all those with ballots are entitled to use them for the big show--The World of Tomorrow.

Pin spot on common man.

GIRL:
Excuse me, which way to the World of Tomorrow?

COMMON MAN:
(Just about to point, when off scene barker's voice is heard.)

BARKER'S VOICE:
Step up--big show--World of Tomorrow!

(As he speaks, crowd turns to look.)

COMMON MAN:
(Pointing) Not that way folks.

BARKER:
(Louder) Right this way, folks. The World of Tomorrow--the Big Show!

Crowd starts going that way.

COMMON MAN:
The Big Show is not there! The Big Show--

BARKER:
(Turns to him) Go away!! (to crowd) Never again

The Common Man

in history will you see such an assembly of freaks and frauds perform under a single tent. What you got to offer?

COMMON MAN:
Not a freak or a fraud in the Place. All I've got to offer is a little paper. (Takes it out of his pocket.) Look, a blueprint of the World of Tomorrow.

BARKER:
This is the World of Tomorrow. (To the cooch dancer) Show them the World of Tomorrow, honey!

The cooch dancer does a bump, and some of the crowd applauds.

BARKER:
(Stops her with a hand, and strikes the gong) That's enough. Step right up and pay your ballot. All got your ballots? (Indicates the dancer) Greatest little ballot dancer ever placed on exhibition. Hurry! Hurry! The Big Show now going on! Greatest Issues on Earth! Monumental Problems brought to this country at great expense from the four corners of the earth. Hurry, hurry, hurry! Your ballot takes you in--we carry you out. Your ballot is good for each and every stall. See the Isolation Troupe--greatest contortion act on earth. Watch them eat their worlds alive. Inside--inside! You pays your taxes and you takes your choice. See the Dance of the Seven Phonies! Philalooloo Nye, the Filibuster--the great double-talk genius captured on Capitol Hill--alive! Watch that world-renowned knife-thrower from Michigan--Clean Cut Clare Hoffman! Throws a knife in the back of the Commander-in-Chief at forty paces! The entire length of the Congressional Gallery! Step right up and cast your ballot to hear the voice of Twerdy Bertie McCormick--Number one on the Berlin Hit Parade!

The crowd stands undecided.

BARKER:
You ain't satisfied? I'll show you more! A sample, a preview, to taunt, tease, and tantalize you! Absolutely free, and without obligation. I give you one look at Nature's Greatest Freak. He's half ham, half fish.

COMMON MAN:
And all elephant!

<u>The Barker hits the gong and the cooch girl takes
her cue and begins to dance as the</u>

BARKER:

(<u>Turning to Barker II</u>) Take over, Doc, they're all
yours. And keep an eye on the untray in the untfray.

BOY:

(<u>Running across stage</u>) Programs! Programs! Get
your programs here! Can't tell Dewey from Hoover without
a program! Get your program. Pictures and numbers of
each and every performer.

BALLOON VENDOR:
Bal-oo-oons! Two cents! Bal-oo-oons!

BARKER II:

(<u>The gentle, caressing type; stops the cooch dancer</u>)
Ladies and Gentlemen, a little closer! A little closer,
please. (<u>To common man</u>) Not <u>you</u>, bub, I have here an
object--a very simple pre-war bottle. In this bottle is the
answer to all your problems. Guaranteed to kill dandruff,
subsidies and the OPA.

FARMER:
Hold your horses, Mister. What's the matter with
subsidies? What's wrong with the OPA?

COMMON MAN:
<u>I</u> didn't ask the question--that farmer asked it.

BARKER:
OK. I'll answer it. Who's for subsidies? The Democrats. Who's for Price Control? Democrats! Who's for
dandruff? (<u>he strikes the gong</u>) You've all heard of George
Washington crossing the Delaware, Ladies and Gentlemen.
In that little boat, on that historic night--mid snow and ice--
there was not one single Democrat present. You can read
the truth in the Congressional Record. The Whole Truth.

<u>As the common man takes a large document from his
pocket,</u>

BARKER II:
(<u>Bangs the gong</u>) Buy a bottle of Boom-times, the
Economic Elixir. Spray a few drops of Dr. Rankin's Ranko

The Common Man 121

on your ceiling, and you can buy what you want! Sell what you want! Charge what you want!

BALLOON VENDOR:
Balloons! Twenty cents!

BARKER II:
And with each and every bottle--without additional charge--we give you Free Enterprise! Who'll start the parade?

FARMER:
Mind another question, Mister?

BARKER II:
I'll answer them all. That's what I'm here for. What's on your mind, brother?

FARMER:
I'd just like to know--how am I gonna get a fair price for my crops without subsidies?

COMMON MAN:
It's the farmer again--don't look at me, bub.

BARKER II:
A fair question. You're an American, aren't you?

FARMER:
Yes, sir.

BARKER II:
And you're a farmer, ain't you?

FARMER:
Yes, sir.

BARKER II:
There's your answer. The American Farmer always got along--and he'll continue to get along--without nobody stickin' his nose into his business.

BALLOON VENDOR:
Balloons! Forty cents!

NEGRO WOMAN:
I have a question--

BARKER II:
Give the lady room--

NEGRO WOMAN:
My husband's a soldier and I live on an allotment. What happens if prices go up and my allotment doesn't?

BARKER II:
Madame--those boys out there in the fox-holes fighting for us ain't complainin'--! (He strikes the gong) Now, if there's no further questions--

BALLOON VENDOR:
Balloons! Ninety cents!

WORKER:
Mind another question, buddy?

BARKER II:
Shoot, brother.

WORKER:
Looks to me like if prices keep goin' up--my dollar's gonna look about as big as a green postage stamp. And without subsidies--

BARKER II:
American, brother?

COMMON MAN:
You left out the 100%!

BARKER II:
Hundred percent! (Turns to the common man) Pipe down!

WORKER:
Hundred percent American. Hundred percent union.

BARKER II:
I'm for unions.

COMMON MAN:
Company unions.

BARKER II:
Company unions! (gets flustered) (he bangs the gong)

The Common Man

A bottle of Dr. Rankin's liquid assets for every shelf. Bigger prices! Bigger profits! More prosperity!

BUSINESS MAN:
    I seem to remember that system in the last war ...

BARKER II:
    Tell the folks what happened, Mister--

BUSINESS MAN:
    In Germany I saw them pay twenty million dollars to mail a letter. I run a business--and if inflation starts coming my way--I'll be getting paid off in pants buttons.

BARKER II:
    That's Free Enterprise, brother.

BALLOON VENDOR:
    Balloons! Two dollars! Beautiful balloons! Only two dollars!

BUSINESS MAN:
    How much?

BALLOON VENDOR:
    Four dollars! That's Free Enterprise!

BUSINESS MAN:
    Free Enterprise hell! That's your kind of Free Enterprise. To me it's inflation! (He sticks a pin the balloon. It explodes and the balloon vendor rushes off stage.)

COMMON MAN:
    Don't look at me--he did it.

BARKER II:
    Don't go way, friends ... (he yells inside) Professor-- send on the magician!

    The cooch girl again takes up her dance. The common man shakes his head as the crowd hesitates, then stays to watch the magician who steps out, in a red-white-and-blue wizard ensemble, a wand in his hand.

BARKER II:
    (Aside to Barker III) Professor--the crowd's restless ...

BARKER III:
 Step closer, folks, and watch me closely. Don't take your eyes off me for a minute.... (he begins to limber his fingers with a deck of cards) Inside, the most miraculous miracle of modern magic is about to be presented for the first time outside Nazi Europe. You have seen the woman cut in two! Now--inside the tent you can witness a nation cut into forty-eight separate and distinct parts. (strikes the gong) First, we separate the body into Jew and gentile. (gong) Then we divide the black from the white. (gong) Then we separate labor and business, soldier and civilian, foreign-born and native American--voter and non-voter. Think of it! We cut off ten million citizens with one swipe of the poll-tax. Six and a half-million no-good, unworthy white Americans, and three and a half million ragged no-good colored brethren.

COMMON MAN:
 Tell me, Professor--are you any relation to the Congressman Hoffman who says--according to the Congressional Record here--that he's an America Firster?

BARKER III:
 America First--yessir, that's the way we do it. We slice up America first--and then carve up the rest of the world. (he strikes the gong) Now, who will be the lucky little character to step up here and watch this amazing piece of sleight-of-hand?

BOOK VENDOR:
 (Moving across the stage) Here it is! The bargain of the century! Five biographies for the price of one! Read the intimate lives of Wheeler, Nye, Reynolds, and Hamilton Fish! All in one volume--Undercover! Undercover!

BARKER III:
 Ah-ha! A man in uniform! Welcome, Soldier ... (to the cooch dancer) Welcome the soldier, honey!

 She does a bump, only embarrassing the soldier, as Barker III turns to the crowd.

BARKER III:
 Folks, here stands a real live nephew of our Uncle Sam, Are you for him, or agin him?

THE CROWD:
> For him!

BARKER III:
> And I'm with you on that. There's ten million of his brothers in armies scattered on battlefronts all over the world. What would you say if I told you there was a monstrous conspiracy against these boys going on at this very minute?

THE CROWD:
> (Ad libs sympathetically.)

BARKER III:
> You know what the administration is tryin' to make these boys do?

CROWD:
> What?

BARKER III:
> Vote!

MAN IN THE CROWD:
> What's wrong with that?

BARKER III:
> We want him to vote, but not the Federal way. That's un-American, unconstitutional, and dangerously convenient.

MAN:
> What's your way, bub?

BARKER III:
> I was comin' to that. I have here a deck of cards put out by the States' Rights Novelty Company ... forty-eight different pasteboards. Each one representing one of our great sovereign states. Pick a card, Soldier. Any one in the deck.

SOLDIER:
> (Picks a card) This is a joker, bub.

COMMON MAN:
> Must be Alabama. They have a poll tax.

BARKER:
> A mere legislative detail. Pick another.

SOLDIER:
> What d'ye know. This one is--a joker!

COMMON MAN:
> North Dakota--Absentee Ballot!

BARKER III:
> A mere technicality--pick another.

SOLDIER:
> Another joker.

COMMON MAN:
> California--Registration Law.

BARKER III:
> Pick another, Soldier--no one's in a hurry. Keep on trying right up till election time.

COMMON MAN:
> You can stop looking, Soldier ... It says here--in the Congressional Record here--that at the time of the last election "Although our armed forces numbered more than five million ... the plain fact is that only 28,051 effective ballots were cast by members of the armed forces ... and this took place under the States Rights system."

WORKER:
> My kid's a sailor!--

WOMAN:
> My son's a soldier!--

BUSINESS MAN:
> My daughter's a marine!--

PRETTY GIRL:
> Hey! My kid brother's a merchant seaman!--

COMMON MAN:
> It's right here in the Record--our Commander-in-Chief says the States Rights Bill is "a fraud on the soldiers and sailors and marines now training and fighting." He says here, "it is a fraud on the American people."

SOLDIER:
  (Grabbing the deck from Barker III) The President's right! They're all jokers! (Throws the cards in Barker's face.)

  Barker III signals the cooch dancer to dance again as the music swells and Barker IV steps out.

BARKER IV:
  Don't go away, folks. We've only just begun. You're not satisfied? You want more? The World of Tomorrow, you say? Well, I'll tell you what I'm going to do. I'll throw in a free peep show. Strip-Tease Landon, Sliding Herbie Hoover, and Humpty-Dumpty Dewey sitting on a fence. See Taffy-Pulling Taft in that great spectacle entitled "Don't waste your bullets on the Japs and the Germans--there's a Democrat hiding in the woodwork." Don't crowd--take your time! Hear Hi-de-ho Nye from Dakota rendering the heart-breaking ballad, "I Lost My Love at Teheran." Watch Little Egypt Wheeler twist her way right out of the Cairo agreement! The World of Tomorrow, you say? Okay! With each and every ballot cast we give a peek into Madame McCormick's crystal ball. Your future read with every vote! (Strikes gong) Step up--join the happy parade! (He strikes gong and Mme. Birdie McCormick steps onto the platform with her crystal globe) Ladies and Gentlemen, I give you the one and only! That peerless, fearless Madame Birdie McCormick and her Crystal Globe! Sees all, knows all, tells all. Reads the Past, the Present Subjunctive, and the Future! Tell me, Madame, what does the future hold?

MME. McC:
  (Looking into crystal ball) I see--I see--

BARKER IV:
  (excitedly) Yes, yes??

MME. McC:
  I see buildings closing down. They're factories! Unemployment!

BUSINESS MAN:
  What about Franklin Roosevelt's 150 billion dollar production plan?

BARKER IV:
  Ssshhh--Madame is in a trance.

MME. McC:
I see soldiers selling apples on the street.

SOLDIER:
Hoover Republican apples.

MME. McC:
I see economic chaos.

HOUSEWIFE:
Roosevelt sees freedom from want, freedom from fear. And Henry Wallace....

BARKER IV:
Don't mention that name--you'll throw Madame off the beam.

MME. McC:
I see labor being regimented.

LABORER:
You mean unionized and strengthened.

MME. McC:
I see <u>bureaucracy</u>!

COMMON MAN:
You mean Democracy, well planned.

MME. McC:
I see Canada!

BARKER IV:
Yes, yes--go on.

MME. McC:
I see Canada invading America!!!

BARKER IV:
Go on, go on, Madame.

MME. McC:
I see America invading Russia!

BARKER IV:
Keep going, Madame, keep going.

The Common Man

MME. McC:
I see Russia invading Mars!!! War, war, war!

BARKER IV:
There's your World of Tomorrow.

COMMON MAN:
That's your World of Tomorrow. No use, bub. Don't you know that the people are hep to your corny show? They aren't going to waste their ballots on your second-hand, hootchie coochie world, your old-hat world, your union-busting, bonus-army-marching, Klan-riding, apple-selling, pistol-packing cartel and to-hell-with-the-people's world. You might as well close up. They won't buy.

BARKER IV:
Well, wise-guy, what are you selling?

COMMON MAN:
I'm not selling anything. I'm just trying to let the people know that there's a real show right around the corner-- a big, new world show. Got the program for that show right in my pocket. (to Crowd) Wanna hear it? It was drawn up at Teheran. Here's what it says: "We are sure that our concord will win an enduring peace ... we look with confidence to the day when all peoples of the world may live free lives, untouched by tyranny, and according to their varying desires and their consciences ..." Signed, Churchill, Stalin, and Roosevelt. That's our show--that's our World of Tomorrow.

The band strikes up offstage, playing "My Country 'Tis of Thee" and the Pretty Girl takes the Common Man's arm.

COMMON MAN:
There's the music--playing for everybody--big man, little man, working man, business man, white man, colored man! The good old song of one people indivisible--sticking together to win the war.... (he jerks his thumb toward the side show) Let them talk about their wars of tomorrow--if we win the war of today, there's not going to be any wars tomorrow! Not if we cast our ballot where it'll do the most good--for Roosevelt and Victory in '44.

LITTLE GIRL:
Who are you, Mister?

COMMON MAN:
 I'm the guy Henry Wallace made famous.

CROWD:
 Oh, the Common Man!

COMMON MAN:
 Yes, I'm each of you, all of you--same as you--the People! And you know what? It's smart to be people!

GIRL SINGER:
 (goes up to Common Man) Mister, you took the words right out of my mouth! (She goes into song ... "It's Smart to Be People.")

--Vol. 30, No. 673 (February 19, 1944), pages 6-8.

THOSE GRIFFITH GIRLS

by Herb Sterne

Mary and Lillian and Dorothy and Constance and Miriam and Mae and Blanche and Carol and Clarine ....

They were the heroines of David Wark Griffith's productions, and the fortunates who had Youth conditioned by silent films will staunchly aver (and with blows as backing, when words are no avail), that never before or since has celluloid imprisoned such an aggregation of beauty, talent and winsomeness as that possessed by "Those Griffith Girls."

Now, there are certain doubters and detractors, men of mean spirit who miaou that such contention is polychromed by prejudice for the past, and that this bewitchment is no proper bewitchment, but rather sheer sentiment distilled from attars of Rosemary and Yesterday. This department, however, hoots derisively at such traducings, knowing full well the potency and the power of the thaumaturgy which the Girls disseminate. And I do not stand as a lone defender in an esoteric joust, for there is sturdy support by word and deed and combative lance from such eclectics of The Field of the Cloth of Silver as Philip Scheuer, DeWitt Bodeen, Dudley Nichols, Jules Dassin, Jean Renoir and Anthony Boucher as to the pulchritudinous and perennial persuasiveness of the demoiselles.

The Griffith Girls set an entirely new fashion and standard in American beauty. They were fragile and gentle and utterly feminine, modeled of the driftwood of dreams, rather than crass reality. Simple and sweet and endearing, they quietly routed and replaced the buxom, statuesque, Gibson symbol in the early years of the century. The Girls compelled nature to emulate Art by making the virginal the vogue, and they reigned as undisputed rulers of the American scene until Mr. Volstead, synthetic gin, and F. Scott Fitzgerald conceived and gave birth to the flapper.

Time, that wormwood even to the Olympians, was temporarily nullified when during seven recent week-ends the "D. W. Griffith Festival" prevailed at the American Contemporary Gallery. The years with their corroded patina were swept aside, and via the projector's glare, and across the screen, trouped the Girls to be seen for what they are and were and will be evermore.

It was heartening and a delight to view Mary Pickford (so recently Gladys Smith), in the process of being borne towards the pinnacle of cinematic celebrity as America's Sweetheart. Mary of the golden curls and beguiling ways with that sad, glad charm so like late afternoon's light slanting through foliage and patterning the sward with shifting counterpoint of brightness and shadow. There were only fragments of her illustrious career presented, briefs from the Biograph days. But beyond The Lonely Villa and 1776 were Rebecca Rowena Randall and Judy Abbott and Sara Crewe, swinging always on the gate of childhood, romping always on a garden somewhere between dawn and sunrise.

And Lillian Gish! A glimpse of her Pre-Raphaelite poignancy in an early sociological melodrama, and then Elsie Stoneman, and Lucy and Anna Moore, dream-figures all, bewildered by, and aghast at, reality. Her frail, golden beauty is poetry made flesh. Her art as delicate and lambent and inferential as any to be projected in the realm of the drama. As great on stage as screen--an accomplishment few have contrived--she is equally effective and intelligent in roles written by Shakespeare and Lottie

Blair Parker, Sean O'Casey and John Oxenford, Chekhov and Thomas Burke, Clarence Day and Dumas, fils. In the listing of superlative artists of the theater and the cinema there is a secure situation, well to the forefront, reserved for the lyrical Lillian.

Mae Marsh, Little Sister of The Birth of a Nation, and the Dear One of the modern episode of Intolerance quite fulfilled one's fondest memories of her work. The sequence of the "Southern ermine" and the death of the child in the former film, and the trial scene and the concluding moments of the latter film, are as encompassing as anything to be culled from histrionic history. And not to be forgotten, although unfortunately not shown in the series: Sands O'Dee and The White Rose.

Constance Talmadge, so blithe, so gay, so utterly delightful as the Mountain Girl of the Babylonian portion of Intolerance. From this role her ascent to stardom was certain. Beyond doubt one of the best light comediennes the screen has fostered, she later effervesced through a series of charmingly capricious comedies, and among the salient were Lessons in Love, The Goldfish and Her Sister from Paris.

Miriam Cooper, brunette and beautiful, was seen as the girl entrapped by crime and circumstance in the modern section of Intolerance. Later, one recalls her brilliant delineations in The Honor System and Kindred of the Dust.

Blanche Sweet, seen only in The Lonedale Operator, presented many notable portraits to the gallery of the photoplay. Probably the highlight of her career was the name part in the silent version of Anna Christie, and other favorite examples of her art include Tess of the D'Urbervilles and The Unpardonable Sin.

Carol Dempster, cold, aloof and seeminging disdainful, was somewhat of a Trilby to the Svengali of Griffith. Her Inga in Isn't Life Wonderful? is a magnificent example of careful coaching, and on one other occasion her glacial presence warmed under the master's guidance in Sally of the Sawdust.

Dorothy Gish, so splendid as the Little Disturber in Hearts of the World and as Louise in Orphans of the Storm unfortunately appeared in none of the films programmed. But one does not forget her in the aforementioned photoplays, or as La Clavel in The Bright Shawl or in such comedic scampers as Remodelling Her Husband and I'll Get Him Yet. Clarine Seymour, too, was slighted in the subjects selected, but nonetheless, a bow to her beauty across the years for the memory of her glowing achievements in The Girl Who Stayed at Home and the South Seas saga, The Idol Dancer.

    D. W. Griffith, as a selector of stars, has never been surpassed, and has rarely been equalled. He dominated his films and his actors as a consummate conductor does members of a symphonic group, and the rhythms of individual performances are most carefully blended with the tempo of individual scenes and that of the photoplay's entirety.

    Griffith created a feminine histrionic hierarchy that absolutely sceptered the screen during the quarter of a century of its Golden Age. His powers of selection are equally potent today, and his ability to pluck a personality from the mob, to mold it and enhance it, remains remarkable. That Hollywood is indifferent to art and genius is hardly a surprise to those conversant with the contemporary format of the celluloid factories. But that, for sheer financial reasons, the industry currently overlooks D. W.'s proved accomplishment in discovering and developing marquee madonnas capable of coining fortunes over long periods of time is, as Lewis Carroll observed of a certain other Wonderland, "curiouser and curiouser."

    A toast, now, gentlemen to "Those Griffith Girls"! Bumpers high to some of the fairest blooms ever to bud and flower in the garden of womankind--To Mary and Lillian and Dorothy and Constance and Miriam and Mae and Blanche and Carol and Clarine....

THE FOOL

by Charlie Chaplin

He looked so old and feeble, and so out of place in the turbulent hustle of the city crowd, that my interest was immediately aroused. He was going in the direction of the Hudson River, crossing the road at Twenty-ninth Street and Madison Avenue. And although he had started with the change of the traffic signal, his progress was so painfully slow that I doubted whether he could make it in time.

His queer, stumbling gait was like one's impeded movements in a dream--his legs operating as though they were extricating themselves from entangled rope. And, as I had anticipated, before he was two thirds of the way across, the signal changed. However, the traffic was not as ruthless as I had for some reason expected, and with considerate slowness it allowed him to pass.

On gaining the curb the old man chuckled and seemed amused by it all. He carried a stick, as well as an old cigar box which he held high in mock triumph. But no one paid any attention. In his exuberance he over-balanced and staggered, but quickly regained himself.

He was an anachronism--this ancient derelict--with clothes that hung on him as on an old scarecrow. His Christ-like whiskers were thin and yellowish white. And beneath an old battered fedora hat, his gray locks furled inward around a sunken neck. His complexion was sickly--translucent, like the inside of an oyster shell. And the features were thin and pointed as though cast from a long illness.

He stood a moment as one having accomplished only a part of his pilgrimage, and looked about him at the milling crowd. As they hurried by, he chuckled and laughed, and made inaudible remarks. There was something ironic in his laughter, I thought--a whimsical resignation of one who knew the torments of hope and its bitter betrayals. He seemed to be mocking them for their hurry, and to be bent on playing the fool. He raised his hat several times to people passing by, but they paid no attention. Nevertheless,

The Fool

his geniality never diminished. And he continued on his way along Twenty-ninth Street towards the Hudson river.

As to what Mecca he was bound, I had no idea. But I intended to find out. I was curious to know more about this old chap and what motivated his journey. So, on the opposite side of the street I followed.

As he hobbled along, hugging his cigar box as an author would his manuscript, he paused occasionally to rest. And while doing so, his legs occasionally buckled. But he would regain them quickly, ignoring the fact. There were no signs of the fool in him now. As he slowly limped along under the eaves of the tall buildings there were only pathos and weariness.

When he came forth into Madison Square, the Metropolitan Tower clock tolled four. The June day was warm and sunny, and a summer spirit pervaded the city square. Precariously he crossed the wide intersection that leads into the park, and entered it. I did not follow, but remained outside at a vantage point where I could see him.

Without hesitation he hobbled up the pathway to a bench. Methodically he placed his stick and cigar box on it, then felt in his coat pocket and produced a lump of bread. Behind the bench numerous sparrows flitted about the green. With a perfunctory air and a dexterity, he nipped off pieces and threw them to the birds. His manner was that of "Milord Bountiful." And he threw with the abandon of abundance. Before his supply was exhausted, however, he was obliged to rest on the bench, throwing the remaining pieces over his left shoulder. When he had finished, he brushed off his hands, took out his handkerchief, wiped his face, wiped his beard, blew his nose, then sat quietly.

Was this the Mecca?--the end of the pilgrimage? Surely, I thought, he has not come all this way just to feed sparrows. There must be other reasons. However, I was not kept in suspense very long, for a moment later he was all primed with renewed energy and was playing the fool again.

At the end of the bench was one other occupant--a lugubrious, old, fat man who, sphinx-like, sat staring ahead of him, his blue puffed hands overlapped on the handle of his walking stick.

"Penny for your thoughts," the old man chuckled. But the fat man paid no attention. A soldier and his girl were passing. Immediately he got to his feet and saluted them, bringing his stick straight up to his shoulder. But they paid no attention.

With a chuckle he picked up his cigar box and ambled off up the pathway. On one of the benches four middle-aged women sat chatting. As he passed them he bowed with embellishment and raised his hat. One of the women laughed and he laughed back, mocking her in a falsetto voice which only made her laugh all the more. With such encouragement he turned and went towards them, but not too close, and without further preliminaries he burst into song:

> I love a lassie--a bonnie Highland lassie,
> She's as pure as the lilies in the dell.
> She's as sweet as the heather--the bonnie purple heather,
> For she's Mary--my Scotch bluebell.

When he had finished he opened his cigar box and gingerly held it out towards them. In it were shoelaces. They smiled, a little embarrassed, and shook their heads. He smiled and shook his head also, his geniality never diminishing, and closing the lid of his cigar box, he slowly ambled away.

It seemed that nothing could affect the amiability of this old clodger--he was so irresponsible, and I began to wonder whether his whimsical antics, his elfish laughter were as profound and as complex as I had thought or whether they were merely the imbecilities of a senile old man. Were I to accost him, I might find out.

Where the paths cross and the branches of the trees almost meet overhead, I caught up with him. "What have you in that box?" I asked.

Tremulously he opened the lid.

"Give me a pair," I said, laying a five-dollar bill on top of the laces.

He looked at the bill, then at me inquiringly.

"You may keep the change," I said brusquely.

Gone was his buffoonery now. In his sunken eyes was a look of bewilderment. He could vie whimsically with the cruelty of life--its loneliness and indifference--but this gift, as small as it was, perplexed him. He was saddened by it.

As I took the laces, he held on to one end of them by way of detaining me. He tried to speak but could not. I thanked him and went my way. Before leaving the park, I turned and glanced back. He was still standing where I had left him, in the center of the pathway. I waved to him, but he did not respond. He just stood gazing after me--a tragic old man with the shadows of the leaves dancing about him like gloom.

--Vol. 30, No. 690 (October 21, 1944), pages 6-7.

D.W.G.: A POET SINGS IN CELLULOID

by Herb Sterne

The artist seeks and discovers his creative outlet in sundry forms. Rembrandt chose paint and canvas as his mode of expression; Donatello, marble; Shakespeare's instrument was words; Mozart's music; and David Wark Griffith selected celluloid.

Griffith not only founded the cult of the cinema, but he was also its major prophet. His accomplishments, salient when seen from the vantagepoint of the present, were miracles when audiences of 1908 compared Griffith's directorial works with those of his contemporaries. Griffith, with the aid of genius and a camera, expanded the confines of the legitimate stage until they included and encompassed the world, and he bestowed a new sweep and dimension to drama as it had been known, theretofore, since its inception in history.

D. W., as producer and director, proved a lyric poet who sang his songs in celluloid. His delicate images have a contoured grace comparable to that of Shelley, Dowson and Keats. In addition, Griffith's visual verse is couched in a language instantly universal, one that all the peoples of the world can read and comprehend at sight.

The films of Griffith are one-man shows, spun from himself, his personality, his individuality. Unlike the majority of standardized motion pictures currently spewed from the studios' assembly lines, his photoplays have a style and distinction that are unmistakable. Beauty and rhythm, an argent idealism, a compassionate apprecation for the simplicities are invariably in evidence. For his masterworks, Griffith evolved a fluid cinematic form that was molded and maneuvered to meet the specific requirements of each individual photoplay.

Today, Griffith is pleased to refer to his films as "experiments." His films were experiments, not only because he was modelling in a new and virtually untried medium, but also because his restless creative urge continually sought unorthodox and additional means of capturing effects and emotion on celluloid. The Griffith films are experiments--but only as all meritorious photoplays are that, whether made during the formative years of the medium, or during the sleek, slick days of 1945 when the technical expression of the craft is so majestically mature and so many of the films are meaningless.

Griffith invented or developed the flash-back, the iris device, close-ups, inter-cutting, parallel plot weaving, the quick-shot and affiliated effects because he felt an urgency to impart the impression of life to his moving fictions. The first American motion picture director to realize the importance of music as mentor to emotion, D. W. had scores composed for orchestras of symphonic size, scores which accompanied his major efforts and italicized the action sequence by sequence and sometimes almost frame for frame.

Of the major works developed under the Griffith aegis, best remembered and perhaps most noteworthy are The Birth of a Nation, Intolerance, Broken Blossoms, Way Down East, Isn't Life Wonderful? and the dialogue film, Abraham Lincoln. In most of these, the producer-director dramatized the natural backgrounds, making them as important and persuasive as the characters who were the protagonists of his plots. Certainly

D. W. G. : A Poet Sings in Celluloid 139

the New England landscapes of Way Down East are an integral merit of the drama, and one remembers them as vividly as Anna Moore, the Bartlett family. And the river, with its shattering ice flow, quite equalled, and often dominated, Lennox Sanderson as the heavy of the plot.

Some of the minor Griffith idylls, less trumpeted and therefore less triumphant through the years, are important for this same strategic molding of nature to the demands of dramaturgy. As tender, lovely sketches in which the countryside contrived to be a successful thematic intensification of the Thespians, A Romance of Happy Valley, The Girl Who Stayed at Home and True Heart Susie are memorable. The bayou country of Louisiana, with its curious, hyacinth-cluttered streams, was caught in all its beauty for The White Rose, a film that has been improperly evaluated and appreciated. And the South Seas, languorous and lovely, have never been so completely captivating on the screen as when netted in celluloid by Griffith for The Love Flower and The Idol Dancer.

As a discoverer and developer of stars, Griffith is paramount in filmdom. He has a way of bringing Wonder to his actors, garbing them in lambent raiment they never can quite match under other managements. It was D. W. who set Mary Pickford's feet towards fortune as "America's Sweetheart." In addition, he sponsored such other performers who became successes as Lillian and Dorothy Gish, Douglas Fairbanks, Mae Marsh, Constance Talmadge, Wallace Reid, Jack Pickford, Blanche Sweet, Henry Walthall, Richard Barthelmess, Robert Harron, Seena Owen, Miriam Cooper, Lowell Sherman, Erich von Stroheim, Bessie Love--the list is limitless.

The impress of David Wark Griffith remains strong on the motion picture even though, to the disgrace of current moguls of the medium, he has been permitted to remain in retirement for some years. One sees D. W.'s influence motivating the creations of Clifford Odets (None But the Lonely Heart), John Ford (How Green Was My Valley, The Long Voyage Home) and in the design and editing and structural solidity which Orson Welles utilized in Citizen Kane, Preston Sturges improvised for The Miracle of Morgan's Creek, and Edward Dmytryk shaped to his needs in Murder, My Sweet. To the sensitive and sentient director of dialogue films, Griffith is as much mentor and model as he was to Rex Ingram for The Four Horsemen of the Apocalypse, and to

King Vidor for The Big Parade and The Crowd during the silent era.

The years have neither dimmed nor diminished the quality and value of Griffith's creations. Time, perhaps, unceremoniously brushes the modes and manners, apparel and moralistic comportment of motion pictures as Time does not tamper with inanimate efforts in art. However, when compared with any photoplays of any year in originality, spirit, texture, design, and what for lack of a more satisfactory word must be termed "soul," those of David Wark Griffith remain securely in the forefront of cinematic accomplishment.

Happy birthday, Mr. Griffith, on January 22. By this time next year may you have completed the direction of a new film for the edification of your multitudes of admirers, one as fine as any of the many with which you have distinguished the screen in the past.

--Vol. 31, No. 696 (January 20, 1945), pages 10-11.

IRIS BARRY: THE ATTILA OF FILMS

by Herb Sterne

> Art is the diamond by which man etches his signature across the window-pane of Eternity.
> --Brahman Proverb.

In literature, sculpture, painting and musical composition it is possible for those who follow the creator's time to turn to the accomplishment and personally assess its worth. The singing stars of the past several decades have been preserved for posterity on wax, and today by grace of a steel needle and a whirling disc it is possible to recreate, much as they were, Garden's Louise, Farrar's Thaïs, Cavalieri's Carmen and the great operatic roles of Caruso.

Unfortunately, with great stage acting of the past, it is possible only to have oblique contact. One may learn of the loveliness and magnetism of the young Maude Adams only through the writings of the drama reviewers of the time, by verbal accounts from the fortunates who saw her, by photographic interpretations glimpsed through the eyes of a still photographer and the eye of his camera. It is impossible for one of 1945 to directly contact Mrs. Siddons or the Kendals; all that remains for us is to have them interpreted to us by sympathetic or antagonistic sources.

The film is, or rather could be, a different matter. Through it, it should be possible to achieve not an oblique but a direct contact with the past. Modes of thought, fashions, the very texture of a vanished age are to be recreated through the glare of the projection apparatus. Since sound, the resuscitation of personality and artistry is perhaps even more precise than was possible with the silent film.

This, of course, is a startling achievement in recapturing the living art of another day when compared to the imperfections inherent in a modern company's revival of a stage play which originally won renown in an earlier era. Those wishful of learning what the Hamlet of Richard Burbage was like receive but little intimation from watching Evans or Gielgud. However, those with a curiosity concerning Laurette Taylor's Peg have a moving shadow portrait to refer to, and the Richard III of John Barrymore lives on, if only in fragment, through the excerpt he recorded by camera and Vitaphone for The Show of Shows.

Although the theory of preserving the precise artistry of a star, a director, a photoplaywright and a production for posterity is feasible and accomplished in film, the questions of accessibility and preservation have not been properly solved. Today, it is rarely possible for a student of the motion picture to see the great achievements of the past reproduced precisely as they were to the acclaim of their particular period. Only one functioning organization, The Museum of Modern Art Film Library attempts to collect and circulate classic cinema in this country. Despite the Rockefeller subsidy, and because of the uninformed obtuseness and arrogantly dogmatic doctrines of the Library's curator, Miss Iris Barry, the organization accomplishes but a minimum of what is properly its function.

Miss Barry's superficial realization of her responsibilities combined with her abysmal ignorance of the American film's worth and import, results in the Library's fragmentary collection which is but ill fitted to aid the student and aesthete in his quest for specific information. Personal reaction, or the lack thereof, seems by the results to be the only yardstick with which the curator is capable of evaluating values. This and the preposterous printed forewords with which the classics of the screen are defaced above Miss Barry's bold signature have rightly won her, in civilized circles, the title of "The Attila of Films."

Many of the prints which the Library screens and circulates are woefully incomplete, although shown as "authoritative" versions which purport to be the films as originally released. Not long ago Mervyn Le Roy was impelled to complain to Miss Barry about the hacked state of I am a Fugitive from a Chain Gang after it was revived locally. In many instances, such as that of von Stroheim's Foolish Wives, the print is so mutilated that the spectator finds it impossible to follow the story line through the mazes of emasculation. Miss Barry disclaims wielding the shears. Even if one were to credit her veracity, it is impossible to condone the lack of knowledge and the lack of concern with values which permit her to libel the creation of an artist and disseminate an erroneous impression of his work to the ages.

Only a segment of the negatives and prints donated to the Library have been made available to the public. Of the work of David Wark Griffith and Douglas Fairbanks which its archives hold, but relatively few examples have been screened. Rumours, some substantiated, point that many of the films have been permitted to distintegrate beyond all hope of rehabilitation. Such negligence has discouraged many creators from contributing their valuable footage to an irresponsible organization. Mary Pickford and Charles Chaplin are but two of Hollywood's artists who have adamantly refused to have their works misjudged and mistreated. It is certainly simple to see why they wish to escape misrepresentation, and Miss Barry's presumptuous and snivelling footnotes with which she delights in festooning films.

While 35 mm prints are shown in the Museum's theater in New York, only raffishly reduced 16 mm versions are available for rental throughout the remainder of the nation. From these prints it is virtually impossible for the student to properly compute the technical qualities of the films, and this pointedly offers insult to the accomplishments of such master pioneer photographers of filmdom as the late Billy Bitzer, and Hendrik Sartov.

Entangled as is Miss Barry in the foreign film, she finds little time to understand or salvage many important aspects of the American motion picture. The serial, a salient and vastly popular attraction in this country from 1913 to 1920, is represented not at all. In a published statement, Miss Barry admits she recovered certain episodes of the Pathé-Pearl White week-to-weeker, The Exploits of Elaine, but she casually adds that the Library will not circulate the exciters because she personally finds them "dull." It is hardly possible to believe the Metropolitan Museum of Art would own and not hang a Rosa Bonheur merely because of the brassy attitude of a member of its staff.

After sitting through the lamentable 16 mm versions of great films which are circulated at outrageous prices by the endowed Library--Anna Christie appears to have been photographed in a monsoon; the last reel of Camille seems to have been steeped in white Rit; Mae West's song "A Guy What Takes His Time" in She Done Him Wrong is as fragmentary as though it had passed through Anthony Comstock's meat grinder--it was recently a privilege to see several motion picture masterpieces as they have been preserved by the artists responsible for their creation.

Mr. Griffith, several weeks ago, ran the lovely Judith of Bethulia made before both The Birth of a Nation and Intolerance, yet photographically superior to the latter if one were to misjudge by comparing the Library's 16 mm prints of those films with this 35 mm Judith. Those of us who saw The Birth of a Nation and Intolerance in the initial showings realize the fallacy, but what of the younkers of today? Griffith's Hearts of the World, which I also had the pleasure of seeing lately on 35 mm, remains intact with its scenes dramatically sharpened by tinted stock, and its entrancingly lensed idyllic love sequences, so beautifully enacted by Lillian Gish and Robert Harron. Miss Pickford, not long ago, gave me the opportunity of viewing Rebecca of Sunnybrook Farm, as well as several short Biograph films, including the delightful Willful Peggy, in which Griffith directed her, and these are a distinct departure from the grainy version of The New York Hat, the only Pickford picture of any importance to the actress' past the Library circulates. Recently, too, at the Chaplin studio, from the comedy master's own vaults, I saw that early experiment in screen sophistication, A Woman of Paris, plus two of Chaplin's shorter triumphs in which he appeared, Shoulder Arms and The Idle Class and these are quite, quite different from the direly duped two-reelers which the Library has exhibited.

It is regrettable that such complete and unchanged films aren't available for general circulation, in all their pristine perfection, for the enlightenment and enjoyment of all who do not feel that the film is only of today, and that it has neither yesterday nor tomorrow.

However, it is perfectly understandable that artists are unwilling to run the gauntlet of the stupidity and negligence which so far has been the policy of the Museum of Modern Art Film Library. There motion picture accomplishment, already assessed by Time and the perspicacious evaluations of such critics as Julian Johnson, Robert Sherwood and Vachel Lindsay, is currently at the mercy of the woeful whims of Miss Iris Barry.

--Vol. 31, No. 702 (April 14, 1945), pages 14-15.

SKELETON

by Ray Bradbury

"Well, I just didn't know it was there until this morning," said the man. His name was Arnie and he swabbed bars and shook cocktails.

"That was a helluva time to find out," said his wife, whose name was Lily. Her work around their house consisted of pyramiding cigarette butts in various containers all day and then carrying them to the kitchen to dump them. After that she started on a new pyramid.

Arnie sat in a big green overstuffed chair, and the smoke from his cigarette made a trembling pattern because his hand was doing the same. "All of a sudden I discovered

Skeleton

it," he said, amazed. He looked down at himself as if every part of his body was a rare piece of ivory carving. "This morning I got a little twinge in my knee, you understand. Then I touched it, felt it." His eyebrows went up, surprised. "There was a bone there!"

"There's always a bone there," said his wife.

"Yeah, but I didn't know it," cried Arnie softly, his cheeks burning. "I didn't know it, and the bone felt funny. It never felt that way before."

"You never looked at it before," said his wife.

"Sure, sure. So this morning I looked at it. You were gone out to the store. I was alone. And I began to wonder." He stopped. "Say--honey, can I--" He asked her earnestly, staring at her. "Can I feel your knee-cap?"

"Oh, for God's sake," she said. "A new approach, yet. In the guise of a bone specialist."

"Can't you see I'm not kidding," he said, and his hands trembled again. "I want to know if everybody's made the same; not just me."

"I'm the same," she said. "Well--almost. A few changes, maybe. Nothing to throw a wing-ding over."

"Anyway," he put it in a picture for her, framed the epic drama in monotone. "I felt my knees. Then I felt my ankles. Then I grabbed my wrists, my arms, my neck, my head! Then I jumped up, like I'd been shot! Christ All Mighty! I yelled! I got a skeleton inside me! Get 'im outa here! A skeleton!"

His wife was looking at him thoughtfully.

"I know what you're thinking," gasped Arnie, lying back in his chair. "You're thinking I'm either drunk or nuts. Maybe I'm both. I had to take a drink. I got a skeleton inside me. Here we go walking around the world, smiling at people, talking at people, shaking their hands, slapping them on the back, and we all got skeletons. Like inside closets. I got to figuring--bodies are closets. We keep bones there."

"What you want to go thinking that for? You're queer."

"Can I help it? I began to shake. I lay on the couch, not able to move. I thought, I got a skeleton in me. One of those things you read about hanging in castle dungeons, with webs on them; or dangling on stone walls clanking in the wind, bronze chains on their wrists and necks. One of those bony, white, horrible things you see all naked on deserts. God!"

"Yeah," said his wife.

"I was scared. I still am. You go walking around taking yourself for granted, not even knowing yourself. And it's like a snap ending on a story, to find you been hiding a regular Mr. Hyde or a Frankenstein inside you."

"You got something there," said his wife.

"So I finally quit shaking at least enough so I could examine myself, and began to feel myself, all over."

"I hope you two live happily ever after," laughed his wife. "You and your skeleton."

"Aw, cut it!" he said, glaring at her. "I felt my ribs, and there they were. Like two big spiders standing over my lungs, pressing 'em in, letting 'em out, pressing 'em in again with their long thin white legs. Oh, baby. And I felt my neck. Feel your neck, Lily. Get hold of the neck bones. That's it. Now, still holding your neck bones, bend your head way back. Way back. Feel? What happens to your neck bones? They go inside somewhere! They're gone! There's nothing to hold your head up but a lot of soft stuff!"

She snapped her fingers away from her neck after the experiment, a shiny light in her grey eyes. "Okay, okay. It's still there. It's inside somewhere. Who cares?"

"And I began to feel how the jaw moves and the joints work. Lord, what I learned. There's bone all around your brain. You read that in school, but you don't think about it, it's just something in a book. And now you find bone around your brain. This damned Skeleton owns us. It holds everything that's important, practically. Your brain, your lungs,

Skeleton 147

your heart. Gee-zuzz! And I began to get scared again. The only good thing about people is they have skin on. Skin and color and hair."

"And a little weight here or there," said his wife, smudging out a cigarette. "But, Arnie, we'd look awful funny, sweets, if we were just skin and fat. Nothing to hold us up."

"I don't want nothing out of a horror novel holding me up!" he cried wildly, hoarsely.

"I can see you're gonna carry on this way a long time," she said, walking over to him. "Honest, Arnie, you're a weird bird. Here." She sat on his lap. "We're all the same. It's okay. Whatever we are it's okay, because that's how we're made. Something's holding me up, too, but it gives me shape, honey. You'll forget about this. You always forget. You get scared of some little thing, the wind at night, the mountains, the snow, and now a skeleton, but you forget, Arnie. It's easy. Here. You want to feel my knee bone? It's the same as yours."

"Can I?" he asked doubtfully, slowly.

"Sure, honey," she said. "Sure."

He touched her knee bone as if it were red hot. It was not red hot. It was only pleasantly glowing and warm.

She leaned against him, kissed him lightly on the forehead, bit his ear tenderly. "You'll forget, Arnie," she murmured, easily. She took the cigarette from his quivering hand, put it in a tray. Then she kissed him on the lips.

Arnie slid his arms, around her. Arnie held her tightly, his hands moving. He kissed her for a long time and then kissed her again.

He stopped trembling.

Deep down inside herself, rich and low, she laughed and sighed with relief, her eyes closed. She pretended to try and get up and go away, but he held onto her and kissed her. She laughed again, warmly, drowsily, deeply. She was proving something to him, she didn't know exactly what, but she was proving it.

A few minutes later her hand, with the skelatinous ghostly white bones inside it, the kind that hang in webbed castles, the kind that lie naked on hot deserts or hang rustling in closets, reached over and clicked out the light.

--Vol. 31, No. 703 (April 28, 1945), page 7.

ALLA BE PRAISED

by Herb Sterne

Friday, the 13th of July of the year 1945, was indeed a dire day for those who cherish the theater: Alla Nazimova was dead.

The death of a great actress evokes not so much sorrow for the actress herself as it does a selfish sadness for ourselves, for we know full well that, forevermore, our evenings in the theater will prove poorer for her passing.

At any period of theatrical history, an actress of Nazimova's artistry would be missed. In this particular period, when a dearth of imposing dramatic talent is but too apparent, her death assumes the proportions of a somber, significant loss to those who conceive of the theater as something beyond a mere evening out from home.

Nazimova, both on stage and screen, achieved an unusual and commanding position. From behind footlights, she popularized Ibsen in the United States. In silent films she commenced, and perhaps completed, an aesthetic trend of production improperly appreciated through the 'Teens, the 'Twenties to today. Despite the fact that her theories of cinema were not commercially feasible, and these financially wrecked her silent film career two decades ago, her artistry is well remembered by the few, while the arid dramatics of many another shadow-actress of the same period have been totally forgotten by the many.

Alla Be Praised

The Russian-born Nazimova, after a continental career as leading lady with Paul Orleneff's company, made her debut in this country in 1905 at the Herald Square Theater, New York, as Lia in The Chosen People. The Brothers Shubert eventually saw her, and presumed that if she could learn the language which is our own, if not their own, a new star would rise on Broadway. Now, drama devotées have many a grievance against the Brothers which, it is fervently hoped, will be settled on The Day of Judgment. However, one thing should shine fair in their favor: they discovered and developed Alla Nazimova for the English speaking stage.

In May, 1906, the actress was signed to a contract to play in English; she commenced taking English lessons on June 23; in November of the same year she made her English speaking stage debut at the Princess Theater, New York, as Hedda Tesman in Hedda Gabler.

Nazimova proved a sensation with both critics and public. In subsequent seasons she added to her repertoire such other Ibsen works as A Doll's House, The Master Builder, Little Eyolf and The Wild Duck. At the Empire, in 1912, she created Ruby Chepstow in J. B. Fagan's adaptation of the Hichens' best seller, Bella Donna. Here, for the first time in that era, appeared an intellectual femme fatale, a siren with a mind as well as a body. In after years, Nazimova was to bring the alluring Mrs. Chepstow to the screen under sundry pseudonyms.

Before the United States entered World War One, Nazimova appeared at the Palace, New York, in War Brides, a highly controversial anti-war skit. Film director Herbert Brenon saw her at the ace vaudeville emporium and instantly realized that she was a personality that would score as well in shadow as in substance.

Brenon was right. Although as a film, War Brides was somewhat hysterical, Nazimova's characterization of the girl who refused to bear a child as fodder for another war succeeded in being both natural and electric. Her pantomime made it simple for the spectator to sense the heroine's thought processes, a procedure which was an astounding innovation at a time when film audiences were accustomed to applaud the "acting" of Valeska Surratt, June Caprice and Violet Mersereau. Both the star and the film were hits.

Nazimova signed a long-term starring agreement with Metro; her first film under the contract was Revelation, based on a rococo novel of mysticism, The Rose Bush of a Thousand Years. The story deals with a model of dubious morality who masquerades as a boy, invades the sanctity of a monastery, and poses, surreptitiously, for the canvas of her artist-lover, as the Madonna. Under the woman's touch the sacred rose bush actually blooms. Then regeneration--Revelation--from the picture of the same name. The starring role was one of violent contrasts, permitting the actress to shuttle from Vice to Virtue with dazzling dramatic virtuosity. The movie public, surfeited for a moment with pretty faces and no talent, acclaimed Nazimova a great actress. Which, curiously enough, she was.

As Nazimova's popularity mounted, so did her ambition to experiment. She had cinematic theories, theories which she gradually infiltrated through her films. A posturized ballet-rhythm, scarcely discernible in Stronger Than Death became stylized symbolism in The Heart of a Child. In Madame Peacock an eclectic artistic stance was achieved which the plain (or garden) variety of movie fan found downright disconcerting. Later, when Nazimova attempted a moderne, impressionistic version of Camille, which had Valentino as a lounge lizard Armand, the ticket purchasers openly rebelled. The sets, by Natacha Rambova, were termed "crazy" by the fan rags, and the fans themselves condemned the film as "stuck-up" for telling its tale in tableaux, rather than in terms of traditional action.

Metro wished to re-sign the star following Camille, but with the stipulation that she should return to ordinary flicker fodder. She refused, founded her own company, and courageously, if unwisely, continued her crusade for Art. She made A Doll's House; it was another failure. This was followed by Salome, an exotic, pantomimic, one-set transposition of the Oscar Wilde drama, with Rambova sets designed after the Aubrey Beardsley illustrations.

Salome not only bewildered movie audiences, it caused them outright outrage. Exhibitors throughout the land reported that patrons demanded their money back after viewing the film. So did Nazimova earn the honor to be the first film star christened "boxoffice poison."

Nazimova then sought to retrace her cinematic steps with Madonna of the Streets and The Redeeming Sin, both of which wilfully stemmed back to Revelation. The public stayed away in droves. She then tried a character role in My Son, which had Jack Pickford and Constance Bennett as boxoffice bait, but the public refused to forget or forgive the earlier affronts to its homespun tastes. Nazimova had no alternative but to retire from the screen.

In an effort to recoup her fortunes, Nazimova mistakenly condescended to stage pot boilers that didn't even simmer. Dagmar failed, and she was driven to the Orpheum circuit, which she toured in such lukewarm schnitzels as Collusion, Mother India, etc., many of which were cheffed by Edgar Allan Woolf, the one-course Shakespeare of the two, three and four-a-day.

Then a lengthy period of retirement, after which Nazimova returned from professional oblivion at the Civic Repertory Theater in a work worthy of her genius, Chekhov's The Cherry Orchard. This proved a triumph, and shortly thereafter she shifted to the Theater Guild where she again scored notably in A Month in the Country, O'Neill's Mourning Becomes Electra, as O-Lan in The Good Earth, and in Shaw's The Simpleton of the Unexpected Isles. Other stage appearances followed, most noteworthy being a revival of Ghosts, which had a brilliant run on Broadway, followed by a successful nation-wide tour.

After a fifteen-year retirement from Hollywood, Nazimova returned to films in 1940, in a film quite curiously named Escape. This was followed by appearances in Blood and Sand, Since You Went Away, In Our Time and as the Marquesa de Montmayor in The Bridge of San Luis Rey. The last two films furnished the actress with her best, if still meager, opportunities in dialogue photoplays.

Nazimova's long and illustrious career was devoted to a personalized ideal of what drama, what acting, should be. As an experimentalist, she was too rarified for popular appreciation in pictures, and (this is pointed out as praise) she was the single film star to both achieve and fail by being intellectual.

--Vol. 32, No. 709 (July 28, 1945), pages 14-15.

JOAN CRAWFORD: ERSTWHILE DANCING DAUGHTER

by Herb Sterne

Joan Crawford is as synonymous with Hollywood as Grauman's Chinese Theater, the forecourt of which holds the footprints of her youth imprisoned in cement.

In a sense, she created the glamor girl as the movies know her today.

The fans worshiped her sequin personality.

But that was not sufficient for Joan.

The Crawford autobiography is to be read from the rigid, pugnacious line of her jaw. Her ceaseless ambition to be canonized in the Temple of Celluloid Thespians has left its contour on the bone structure of her face. This is denoted in bold relief on Djey Owens' sculptured and frankly retrospective head, which presents Joan with the long-bob, the semi-circular eyebrows, and the mouth vastly distorted by makeup which marked an earlier manner of the star.

In her pursuit of greatness, Joan has presented an assortment of appearances to the camera, but only one talent. She has frequently changed her makeup, the color of her hair and its arrangement, her diction, and her marital status, in hopes of achieving her goal.

The fans best liked her as they first applauded her, in Our Dancing Daughters. They wanted Joan as the headlong girl from the right side of the tracks who would dive into a swimming pool ('though fully clothed by Adrian) at the drop of a champagne glass. Or, they wanted her as the girl from the wrong side of the tracks who soared to a Park Avenue penthouse, either with or without benefit of clergy.

In either of these assignments, Joan was what at dear old pre-Hitler Ufa, we termed a schlag. But whenever Joan discarded personality in order to "act," Marion Davies would outgross her at the boxoffice.

Joan Crawford: Erstwhile Dancing Daughter 153

Joan Crawford, the soignée star of today who broods with taut attention while Toscanini conducts a symphony, and who is aggressively vain of being able to differentiate between a Picasso and a Maxfield Parrish, is somewhat different from the Shubert chorine who arrived in Hollywood twenty years ago and promptly cornered the local market in Charleston and Black Bottom contest cups.

It required two decades and three husbands to transform Joan into the great lady she desired to be. Her determination to be hailed as another Duse remains unsatisfied. But "Jaw" Crawford is still in the celluloid ring, and punching. Mayhap she will still make it.

Within the span of two decades, Joan deliberately cut and tailored a new personality, a new point of view for herself. The vital, eager and entirely electric lass who arrived at M-G-M in 1925 has disappeared as completely as the Volstead frame in which she flourished. In her place is a chi-chi matron with a conversational comprehension of modish intellectual and artistic topics, one so poised, so genteely restrained, so "right," as to impart the impression that each morning, on awakening, her first impulse is to memorize passages from the latest edition of Emily Post. All that remains of the girl who danced in the rear line of the Mistinguett musical, Innocent Eyes, is a penchant for noticeable dress. Whenever Joan appears in public she is frocked as she believes her fans wish her to be frocked, and this is something between the style favored by Valeska Surratt, circa 1915, and that which Cléo de Mérode decided to assume when she first cast sheep's-eyes at a Throne.

Joan's natural, uninhibited personality was vital and completely photogenic. From Sally, Irene and Mary to Letty Lynton she gave the public what was her own, and the fans were completely enchanted. She did much to lend impetus to the middle and late years of the Jazz Age by her delineations in The Taxi Dancer, Our Dancing Daughters and Our Modern Maidens.

Joan became a star and when sound arrived, in 1929 she successfuly entered the audible medium by introducing a song, "I Got a Feelin' for You," in The Hollywood Revue. Joan's voice was husky, natural, and it completely matched her photographic image. About this time Joan married young Fairbanks. Rumor had it that Doug Sr. and Mary Pickford were somewhat less than ecstatic about the match, and the report gained credence when the famed pair failed to attend the nuptials.

Joan's struggle towards what she considered the heights is to be traced to this time. According to legend, she began spending long hours studying Juliet with a drama coach, grand opera arias with a vocal instructor, and Doug Jr. is reputed to have overwhelmed his spouse by revealing that there were books besides those of the check and savings variety.

This, of course, was none of the public's affair, as Joan continued to appear in such highly suitable vehicles as Dance, Fools, Dance, Grand Hotel, and Laughing Sinners. Her Mary Turner, in a version of Veiller's Within the Law released as Paid, was excellent. And the musical montage at the piano in Possessed, during which Joan sang "How Long Will It Last?" and several songs in foreign languages to illustrate character development, remains memorable.

In 1932, Joan had two failures: her marriage to young Doug, and her appearance in Rain. As Sadie Thompson, Joan obtained what she decidedly believed to be her great acting chance. And she acted. The critics pounced. The public stayed away. Rain was a comprehensive washout. It must be admitted that the star had considerable competition in the memory of Jeanne Eagels' luminous enactment on the stage, and the hearty characterization which Gloria Swanson had proffered in the silent film. But whatever excuses one manufactures for Joan, it is impossible to deny that she needn't have spewed forth all her recently acquired culture by playing a damsel of the Smoke Street circuit as though she were Jeanne Francoise Julie Adélaide Récamier presiding over a salon in the south seas.

When Joan returned to M-G-M from her disastrous loan-out to U.A. (and how a couple of stockholders in the latter company must have chuckled, even though it was expensive merriment!) Today We Live displayed that the star was still suffering from delusions of histrionic grandeur. Her Culver City bosses, fearful of losing a valuable box-office property, cast her in Dancing Lady. Once again she was Irene and Diana; and good too, it should be added. Sadie McKee and Chained also swathed her in suitable personality parts.

Joan Crawford: Erstwhile Dancing Daughter

Miss Crawford became Mrs. Franchot Tone, and now she determinedly turned from being a personality, at which she was expert, to being an actress, at which she was not. Forsaking All Others, The Gorgeous Hussy, The Last of Mrs. Cheyney, The Bride Wore Red--. Just about the time when the lady had convinced one that nothing more catastrophic had been offered as entertainment since the Cherry Sisters toured as a quartette, Joan made Mannequin, in which she acted not at all and again proved very charming indeed. By the time she appeared in The Ice Follies of 1939, all was artifice. Her accent was strictly Miss Finch's School, and the numbers she sang in the film were so woefully "operatic" they were hacked from the footage following the preview. Acetate recordings of the songs have become collectors' items, and they must be heard if one is to appreciate their full, if lamentable, fame.

In 1939, Joan ceased being Mrs. Tone. In 1942, she married Phil Terry. When last glimpsed on screen and off, Joan was still determinedly being an "actress."

Recently, I viewed a revival of Our Dancing Daughters and there is ample cause to regret the disappearance of the natural, vivacious girl whose streamlined loveliness set a new and titillating style in personality performers.

A strong jaw, which denotes courage, defiance and pugnacity, is no doubt a notable asset.

Joan still wishes to be an actress. Miracles have happened. Perhaps one would happen to Joan if she would only relax and be herself.

--Vol. 31, No. 713 (September 22, 1945), pages 6-7.

ELECTRIC SHADOWS

by James Wong Howe

The Chinese have had popular "screen shows" for two thousand years. A white cloth stretched between two bamboo poles was set up at night in the market place. An oil lantern lighted the screen from the back and experts manipulated their life-like, translucent, colored puppets. There were shadow plays and dramas. There was dialogue and music and color, and always an interested audience. These shows were called "lantern shadows." The modern motion pictures are called tien ying, "electric shadows."

The Chinese "electric shadow" industry, although potentially important, is small and weak, as might be expected in an industrially undeveloped country. China, predominantly agricultural, with almost its entire industry concentrated so near the seaboard that it was quickly destroyed by Japan in 1932 and again in 1937, has been neglected as a market and its resources have never been exploited. China represents one fifth of all mankind, and its future is of vital importance to the whole world, whether its future is to be that of a backward, exploited country, or a developing, democratic nation.

Motion pictures, with their possibilities for education, culture, entertainment, will be an exciting part of post-war China. But they cannot develop without an accompanying development of other industries. As railroads and modern methods of communication extend into the interior, and language barriers are broken down and standards of living rise, interest in movies will develop, theatres will be built, and, above all, there will be that extra hour of leisure and that extra piece of change without which you cannot go to the movies.

Hollywood has so dominated the international market that it may seem premature to discuss the possibilities of film production in countries unheard from before the war. But with the world made small and accessible these possibilities are taking on reality. Treated with intelligence, this prospect, it seems to me will be interesting and

Electric Shadows 157

profitable for all concerned rather than disturbing. But
immediate gain has a way of getting in the eye like a cinder, to say nothing of getting in the heart like a stone. A
war or a soft peace, for instance, may appear to a few to
be more financially desirable than considerations of long
term human profit. The majority of people may see more
clearly than that. The important thing is not only to see
but to do.

If the age of the common man is upon us we must be
proud of our role as world citizens, and contribute in the
way we know best--through our work. Since our work here
in Hollywood is movies, naturally we think in those terms.
Of course, with a little further thinking, it is easy enough
to see how closely connected pictures are to other phases of
living.

Before the war there were only a few studios in China
and not quite 400 theatres, most of these concentrated in the
coastal cities. They showed 85% American films, 15% native,
Russian, French and British. There were a few machines
of their own invention, but the bulk of material, including
film, came from the U.S.A. The advent of sound was more
of a set-back than a help because of the incredible language
difficulties. Dialects change from province to province, and
are not understood outside their own immediate areas. There
is no universal language in China, although Mandarin and
Cantonese are two of the largest dialects. Government decree made Mandarin the national dialect and that became the
language of the films. However, a small percentage was
permited in Cantonese because actually aside from the northern cities, the income came largely from the southern cities,
the Malay States, Hawaii, and cities of the United States with
large Chinese populations. With the exception of students
and officials who may be from either north or south, the
emigrating Chinese are southerners, speaking Cantonese.

The industry was not taken seriously nor treated
with respect, either as a field for investment or as a career.
Its financial resources depended on the entertainment concessions and on a few adventurous individuals returning from
the States. The studios managed to develop several stars,
the best known being Butterfly Wu whose pictures came to
enjoy long runs in the cities. The pictures were of a poor
quality in every sense, for the most part imitative of the
worst in our own films. All the characters were rich, carefree souls, with no relation to anything in China or in life,

except, perhaps, a frivolous minority in the few worldly cities. But the great bulk of Chinese dramatic material was left untouched. The make-up of Chinese actors to represent Americans and Europeans, by the way, was astonishingly good except for a little trouble around the eyes.

With the war, things began to change. Fifteen hundred film people joined the long trek inland by river boat and foot. They took what equipment they could with them. In Chungking, to escape the bombings, laboratories, editing and storage compartments were built in tunnels thirty feet below ground. Sound stages were on the surface. At the sound of an air raid, equipment was quickly carried into the dugouts. The destruction of an important item sometimes interrupted shooting for days. When the water supply was cut off, as in 1939, these people carried water from the river up a long hill and poured it into a reservoir. All film had to come from America by long, crude, painful means of transportation. Every inch of that film became precious. It could be used only for the most meaningful purpose.

In Japanese-held territory theatres were confiscated and former sound stages were turned into stables by the enemy. In Free China one hundred and twelve theatres showed Chinese, American and Soviet films. The greater part of the workers and stock in the industry, went to the various government projects turning out military and propaganda pictures. This was a hard life. Many of the units went to the sprawling fronts. They traveled by truck, mule, camel and afoot, sometimes over roadless areas. They went to villages behind Japanese lines, and even 3,000 miles in Inner Mongolia, where people saw movies for the first time. Farmers and soldiers saw the films and found in them a universal language, a way to knowledge and a means of communication with the unknown outside world.

This vast circumstance reveals the power of the screen in such a telling way that its potential for good seems hardly to have been touched. But just imagine pouring into these fertile, eager minds the hokus-pocus that passes for and is defended as entertainment! Here, I'd like to say that it seems to me that too great a distinction has been made between art and entertainment. The same argument goes on in China as in America. In China it centers on the difference between Soviet and American films. It is a revealing comment on us all that we may not find entertainment and pleasure in the good, the serious, the thoughtful, and must believe that only the light and superficial is entertaining. Actually one without the other lacks appeal; they should be inseparable. No one would deny that some films stress one quality more than the other. But our own propaganda and educational documentary war films and those of other nations have not failed in their entertainment value, but have combined the two necessities well. The same is true of serious drama. A good musical, too, may propagate certain ideals and enrich our taste in music. A gay comedy often satirizes things that should be held up to ridicule.

Motion pictures will play an important role in the rebuilding of China, more important than the role we are used to associate with our own films. For one thing, they will be the strongest factor in breaking the enormous spoken language barriers which divide China.

If the movement to Romanize the writing of Chinese gathers enough force, people everywhere will learn to read and write. Many of us here do not realize that in China reading and writing are the luxury of the scholar, and that the majority of people are shut out from this means of communicating thought. Character-writing may be beautiful and picturesque but it serves only the few. The possibilites of films in education, in sanitation, in health, in cultural and technical learning, in visual knowledge of all kinds are almost limitless.

China, with the growth of its own industry, will turn from western imitations to her own rich sources of drama, to the inexhaustible materials of her ancient colorful history, to the experiences of China's years of war and to the stories of her own original young writers. Examples of what these young writers are doing can be seen in two recent novels out of the war years which have been republished in America, Village in August by T'ien Chün, and Rickshaw Boy by Lau Shaw. Other current themes would deal with changing China, the growing freedom of women, for instance. China has as many types of people, and as great and varied a wealth of scenic background and climate, as America or the U.S.S.R.

An important field in which China and the United States will cooperate, I think, is the development of the technical branch of motion pictures. The United States is far ahead in techniques and technicians, much equipment and many technical workers will be in demand in China. China must look toward Hollywood for help until her own workers are trained. China will have to use a great majority of foreign films to supply her vast potential audience. She must also develop her own industry on a large scale. With a population of more than 400 million, it is sensible to believe that the U.S. will profit rather than suffer by the development of China's film industry.

The Chinese government is now preparing to furnish hundreds, perhaps thousands, of 16 mm. projectors and screens for the running of educational as well as entertainment films throughout the country. Hollywood can expect to sell many regular productions reduced to 16 mm., as well as an exchange of documentary films which will increase the mutual understanding of our countries. Incidentally, I have been talking for years about the coming of age of the 16 mm. film. Now, stepped up by its brilliant use in the war, it is here, and with even vaster promise than I imagined. The documentary film, so often buried by its critics, is more alive than ever and will find new fields and new uses. It will be made by governments and by professionals, as well as experimenting amateurs, to whom so much of the credit for its present excellence belongs.

When we can see which way the winds are really blowing in the Far East, we will be able to speak in more definite terms of the future of China. One thing we do know is that there is a tremendous movement of peoples fighting against age old burdens of oppression from within and without, towards a democratic way of life. Whatever halts they may suffer on the way, they have shown a sure advance within Kuomingtang China and even more so in the Yenan areas. This advance will continue as inexorably as a tide until China again takes her place among the nations. It is not to be hoped that her civilization of the past, once so splendid and since fallen into ruin and decay, will be restored, but rather that a new civilization will be permitted to develop and mature in freedom. An independent, modern China is an essential factor in the peace and progress of the world.

--Vol. 31, No. 714 (October 6, 1945), pages 8-9.

CARLTON MOSS: OUR COVER BOY

by Dalton Trumbo

It is very difficult to write a piece about someone for whom you have real affection. It is even more difficult when this person happens to be a distinguished man and a fine citizen. For then you are likely to go off the deep end and eulogize him to the point where the reader gets bored and says hell, nobody can be that good. In writing such a piece you have to be objective. You have to rule out your emotions entirely and confine yourself to a bare recital of facts strung together in dignified fashion. This is what I am going to try to do, as follows:

The young man whose photograph you see on Script's cover is named Carlton Moss. He is a resident of this community and for this reason alone you should know something about him and his work. He is one of the most talented writers in the United States. For seven years he was a writer and actor for a community forum over station WEVD. He is the author of Prelude to Swing, the original production of which was done by the Federal Theatre. He was director of the Harlem Federal Theatre. His monograph on Negro Music Past and Present is an established reference work. For William Grant Still, the composer, he wrote the book for the opera, Blue Steel.

During the war he served as a consultant to Secretary Stimson and as information specialist for the Information and Education Division of the War Department. He wrote and acted in many War Department films, including what I believe to be the greatest documentary of the war, The Negro Soldier. His most recent War Department documentary is Teamwork, shortly to be released, the material for which he gathered on an extensive tour of the ETO. He is now an associate in United Films, producers of progressive documentaries. He is also delivering a series of lectures on "The Negro in the News," and is preparing a series of radio programs on the same subject. He is a member of the American Veterans Committee and the United Negro and Allied Veterans of America. He sits on the executive boards of the Hollywood Independent Citizens' Committee of the

Arts, Sciences and Professions. This is his record to date, and he is still very young.

Reading this over, it doesn't seem to give a very clear picture of Carlton Moss. It's objective enough. It certainly doesn't go overboard. And yet somehow....

Very well. To continue about him objectively. As you can see from his photograph he is a Negro. This means that he has more melanin in his skin that I have, and that I have more hair growing from my skin than he has. This doesn't seem to be a very profound difference--this having more melanin and not being quite so hairy--but because of it the American Negro has become one of the most oppressed people on earth. He is, in a good many states, denied the right to vote but granted the right to pay taxes. He is forced to live apart from others of the human race in ghettos. He is obliged to travel separately, like an animal or a corpse. His income is below the national level and his rent is above it. His children receive less education than white children, more of them die in infancy, more of their mothers die in childbirth. His disease rate is higher than that of whites, and so is his death rate.

In the last sixty years 4,708 of his fellows have been lynched in democratic America, the most popular methods being shooting, flogging, hanging, disemboweling and burning. Only this winter in Columbia, Tennessee, a young Negro veteran made the mistake of defending his mother against the assault of a white shopkeeper, and provoked a kind of American Lidice, in which armed whites, accompanied by police, invaded the Negro community and arrested scores of Negroes, two of whom were murdered during their period of imprisonment. Today, thirty men are on trial in Columbia for their responsibility in the insurrection. A number of them are veterans. The men on trial are not the whites who committed the assault, but the Negroes who resisted it. They are being tried before an all white jury. They are sampling democratic justice in a country where--

Wait a minute. This isn't being objective. This is getting to be propaganda. Pretty soon I'll be talking about the F.E.P.C. and the Anti-Poll Tax bill, and this piece will lose all of its objectivity and most of its elegant tone. For it is always claimed by the newspapers and the police that people who complain about the treatment of Negroes are precisely the ones who stir up riots and cause all the trouble.

Carlton Moss: Our Cover Boy

I wouldn't want to stir up trouble for the Negroes just by writing a piece about a friend. They have enough trouble already.

Getting back to Carlton Moss, my friend and neighbor. I am reminded that the other day a man came to my house representing a group of prominent Beverly Hills citizens who were circulating a petition which would place restrictive covenants barring all but Caucasians from the block in which I live. I read this list of sponsors very carefully, and found there the name of an actor who, like a good many people in motion pictures, has risen to affluence from the nickels and dimes paid into the box office by working people, including, I daresay, Negroes. It struck me so oddly that I began to laugh, and this man they had hired to pass the petition around said "What are you laughing about?"

So I said, "You go and tell this actor that I am laughing about him sending this kind of a petition around." Because, I said, it wasn't so long ago that actors couldn't buy property in nice neighborhoods either. As a matter of fact, I said, actors weren't even allowed inside the city gates after sunset, and nobody would be caught dead eating at the same table with one of them and they couldn't be buried in holy ground, and it was against the law to speak of them as Mister Actor or Monsieur Actor or Herr Actor. Just the name, and no title. And then, I said, along came that French Revolution with all its wild talk about equality. And pretty soon actors were getting inside the city gates after sundown, and even finding beds. They were getting buried in holy ground like merchants and civic boosters and everybody else. People started saying Citizen Actor or Monsieur Actor. And finally it got so that people were even eating at the same table with them. Apres that le deluge. You go and tell that actor, I said to the man, that I'm getting up a petition too. And if he'll sign mine, I'll sign his.

But about Carlton Moss--and this piece is about him-- I find it difficult to tell you exactly what kind of man he is. And yet I know him well. I know his sense of humor, which is oblique and sharp and filled with a kind of joy which imparts itself to all who are with him; I know that he is the most completely integrated person I have ever met; I know his tremendous capacity for work and the zest that goes with it; I know his fine ability to put people at their ease, his rich qualities of friendship and neighborliness and yet....

It's always about this time of night that somebody gets up in the back of the hall and hollers, Yeah, but how would you like your sister to marry One?

This happens to be a question I can deal with, because when I was a lot younger I had an unmarried sister. She was a pleasant, good-looking girl with just a touch more melanin in her skin than I had. And naturally I did a good deal of brooding about What if my sister marries One?

I got to thinking, she is such a fine girl and so handsome and such a Caucasian that sure as hell one of Them is going to marry her. I was so sure it was going to happen that the only question in my mind was which One will it be? Every time I saw a Negro on a street car or walking down the sidewalk I watched him carefully, knowing that in his heart he was resolved upon marrying my sister. Then I got to thinking about all the Others who had the same idea--Chinese and Japanese with more carotene in their skins and practically no hair at all; Indians and Hindus and Melanesians and Micronesians and Polynesians and Indonesians and Malayans and Sikhs and Arabs and Africans and Pygmies and Bushmen and-- good God!--hundreds of millions of Them, a good three-quarters of the men on earth, all of Them colored in one way or another, all of Them lusting and leching and yearning and conniving to marry my sister!

This went on for a year, maybe two years, with nothing happening, I could not understand why none of Them came around, nor even followed her home from work. I was impatient to face the crisis and have done with it. I got sullen about it. I thought, what the hell is wrong with Them anyhow? Every time I saw one of Them I would think to myself, <u>oh-ho</u>, so you don't want any part of my sister, I suppose <u>she</u> isn't <u>good</u> enough for you, eh? I began to nag my sister about maybe a different makeup, and wouldn't her hair look better if it were more wavy. She had no idea what I was trying to save her from, so naturally she gave me curt answers.

When I perceived there was no gratitude in her at all, I came to a conclusion which has been satisfactory to me ever since. I washed my hands of the whole matter. I decided that maybe it was her business whom she married anyhow, and that marriage depends on mutual consent, and that most people tend to marry whomever they damned well please, and so perhaps I'd better worry about myself for a change. I began immediately, have found it a full time job ever since. Only just last night I--

I seem to have wandered off the subject again.

I may as well face the truth of it: I just can't write objectively about Carlton Moss.

--Vol. 32, No. 734 (July 20, 1946), pages 8-9.

THE OUTLAW RIDES AGAIN

by Louis L'Amour

If Howard Hughes intends to continue producing pictures like The Outlaw, his studio had better do something about research.

At any moment now I am expecting to walk into a theater to see Ulysses S. Grant attacking the Maginot Line, or Lydia Pinkham doing the Salome dance with the head of Senator Bilbo.

To anyone with the slightest knowledge of Western history, this most recent display of Western lore is painful, to say the least.

If I were a relative of either Pat Garrett or Doc Halliday I'd sure sue somebody.

Of course, the following points may seem unimportant:

Pat Garrett did not kill Doc Halliday.
Doc Halliday does not lie in Billy the Kid's grave.
There is no evidence that Halliday ever knew either Billy the Kid or Pat Garrett.
Pat Garrett was not the weak, frightened character he appeared in the movie.

Nobody ever shot any holes in the Kid's ears and, as that proved a man a coward, the Kid would have shot his own mother rather than have it happen.

If Howard Hughes wants to do a western, why not do one entirely fictional instead of taking the facts of known lives and distorting them out of all reason?

All credit to the cast. They did a good job with their material. From my seat, Jane Russell's mammary display was adequate. Jack Buetel looked youthful enough for Billy the Kid. Walter Huston, as always, turned in a fine performance, as did Thomas Mitchell.

If Hughes wanted to do the story of Billy the Kid, why did he not use the real story, which is packed with dramatic dynamite? If he needed a deadly gunman as the friendly antagonist of Billy, why not the man who was actually that?

I refer to Jesse Evans. Evans and the Kid stole horses together, fought Indians together, and gambled together. Evans was, by reputation, fully as dangerous with a gun as Billy. Then, in the Lincoln County war, they took opposite sides. Three times during the months that followed they met under tensely dramatic circumstances where the slightest wrong word would have ended in a shoot-out.

Why junk a valuable, interesting, exciting story to distort the facts? Doc Halliday, known as "the most cold-blooded killer in Tombstone" was the son of a fine old Southern family. He came from Georgia, and, for a brief time, was a dentist in Dallas. He met Wyatt Earp, thereafter his greatest friend, in West Texas. They were in Dodge together, later they rode together in Tombstone, and when they left Tombstone, they left together.

During his life he offered odds of eight to five that he would die with his boots on in a gun fight. He would have lost.

A lifelong sufferer from tuberculosis, he died in Cottonwood Springs, Colorado, and it struck him as so amusing that he should die in bed, his last words were, "This is funny!"

The Outlaw Rides Again

He was a pale man with ash blond hair. Intelligent, witty, and with a hot temper, under fire he was as cold as ice. He always stood (as many gunmen did) with his side toward an enemy when he fired. As he was unusually thin due to his illness, he made a small target. While he was an excellent shot with a pistol, he usually used a sawed-off double-barreled shotgun. In other words, when he shot, he shot for keeps!

Pat Garrett, instead of being the weak, sloppy character offered by the movie, was a successful rancher and famous peace officer. He was six feet four inches tall, very fast with a gun, and he killed Billy at Fort Sumner; shot him in Pete Maxwell's bedroom there. Several years ago I was shown Billy's grave by an old Indian woman. At that time the grave was abandoned, known to few, and unmarked.

In the past few years I've written a number of western stories, and in the past five months, have sold six western shorts and two full length novels of the west, aside from a few other things, and have been a student of western history since I was a youngster. The trouble with pictures of this kind is that thousands upon thousands of people know no better.

It is never a good thing to underestimate one's audience, and Hughes is guilty of that. The facts of this story are known, to most of the population of New Mexico, Arizona and Texas. Accounts of the doings of the Kid and Doc Halliday have been written in many western magazines, and biographies of the Kid are on the market at present.

Aside from the fact that it reflects on the historical integrity of all films and is therefore distinctly harmful, it is absolutely useless and serves no artistic purpose.

A great deal has been written about the lengths to which a producer will go to make a picture authentic; certainly, this was a bad slip-up. The ear-shooting episode was impossible from the standpoint of Billy's character. The scene where he makes his bed in the moonlight was absurd. Too many men wanted to kill Billy for him ever to do that. The final wrong touch was Billy's taking the girl up behind him when Halliday's horse was available. No man in his right mind ever started off on a long ride in Apache country with a horse carrying double.

But of all this composite of mistakes, the worst was dragging Doc Halliday into the story at all. He had no place there, wasn't needed, and as I've said, didn't die that way.

Dramatic necessity may sometimes demand the distortion of minor details. There was no such necessity here. The picture could have been done much better and remained historically accurate and authentic as to character.

--Vol. 32, No. 736 (August 17, 1946), page 8.

SCREEN

by Lillian Gish

The main concern of actors in the silent film was simply--how to be articulate without words. Today, with the aid of dialogue, the demands made upon actors are less strenuous.

Where once we tried for a characterization in pantomime, through an odd walk, strange mannerisms or pieces of business, now one spoken sentence is able to convey an entire character: hence the modern tendency of the screen to follow the Gerald DuMaurier stage school of casual acting.

On the silent screen, the story, told in terms of physical action, led directly to a final emotional climax, such as the prize-fighter beating his child to death in Broken Blossoms, the film Mr. Griffith made from Thomas Burke's The Chink and the Child. Then, we acted out the narrative and climactic situation as completely as we could for the audiences. Today, in talking films, the tendency is to lead up to a dramatic moment, and the climax is left to the audiences' imagination.

For example, a bride seeing her husband shot dead before her eyes simply turns her back to the camera and runs away into the distance as the camera fades out. Such a scene makes little demand upon the emotions of screen actors today, and in this current, casual school it is all too simple for the spectator to confuse an absence of emotion for restraint. This is due not to the lack of histrionic ability, as there are more and better actors now in Hollywood than ever before in its history. It is, perhaps, due to the fact that great scenes in motion pictures are not easily written. It could also be due to the fact that to play emotional scenes of size and persuasion before the camera not only takes high imagination and careful thought, but also much time spent in preparation and rehearsals.

The Hollywood of recent years seems to have lost sight of the value of rehearsing the story with the actors who are to play the parts. When D. W. Griffith paid the then huge sum of $165,000 for what we thought an old-fashioned play, Way Down East, he knew he could not afford to waste money in making a picture that would be over-length, with many good scenes left on the cutting-room floor. So we rehearsed constantly for eight weeks. The last half of that time the cameraman and cutter were present with stop-watches, carefully timing each scene to the split second, so all of us concerned in the production knew exactly how long we were to have to convey what we had to do in each separate scene.

I was often criticized for jumping in and out of rooms in the old silent films. This was always done to allow enough footage to play scenes without wasting film on entrances or exits, which are not as important in pictures as they are in the theater.

These long weeks of rehearsals saved thousands of dollars that might otherwise have been wasted in excess footage, and enabled the actors to discover how important it was to play with the intensity and unction that give a film vitality and hold the interest of an audience.

A few weeks ago an exhibitor told me that Way Down East had broken box office records in Pittsburgh for all time. Never, before or since, has any film in its first run in that city played to more than a quarter of a million dollars, as did Way Down East.

If you have seen Thornton Wilder's play, Our Town, in the theater, you will know exactly what our rehearsals were like, as we tried to give a completely articulate performance.

Now and again, we would be asked to run through the entire story in silence. (Mr. Griffith was ever watchful for anything that was not effective on celluloid.) But most of the time the rehearsals would be with dialogue improvised by the players. During these rehearsals the actors talked constantly, ad libbing lines that fitted the action. Many of our speeches were used later in sub-titles in the finished film, for most of them were taken down in writing by a secretary for the cutter, for Mr. Griffith never used a script, and these notes were the cutter's only means of following the story when assembling the film.

When speech first came into the movies, I felt it was a mistake, as it not only created the barrier of language, thus making Hollywood pictures understood only by the English-speaking peoples, but it also slowed down the telling of stories which had heretofore been projected through emotion and action. I thought motion pictures would benefit more by marrying with music rather than speech.

Not until I saw Dudley Nichols' The Informer did I realize how effective, though not as universally understood, the combination of the three--music, pantomime and speech--could be.

Nichols understands the value of pantomime. He has such high regard for it that whenever a script of his breaks into words, it is with an economy of words so potent as to enhance the drama.

Full-length rehearsals of complete screenplays would allow the writers of today to hear their dialogue from the mouths of their characters. It would help the actors to integrate the words and characters. And it would aid the director to sense the weak and strong points of his story and judge the tempo in which it should be played.

All of this combined, I am sure, would make for better films, with less cost that the present methods, where an actor, however competent, finds himself more concerned when before the cameras, with remembering the next line than with the character he is playing. The net result often is that there is no characterization, not to mention the fact that all action is slowed and the picture is robbed of tempo.

Mechanically, the motion picture has mounted steadily in technical perfection. When the mechanical expertness is equalled intellectually and spiritually, America may very well be proud of the part it has played in fostering this, the youngest of the arts.

--Vol. 32, No. 738 (September 14, 1946), pages 10-11.

INDEX TO CONTRIBUTORS

Richard Sheridan Ames	24
Ray Bradbury	98, 144
Eddie Cantor	63, 111, 113
Charles/Charlie Chaplin	27, 41, 80, 82, 108, 117, 134
Agnes George de Mille	6
Philip Dunne	64
Lillian Gish	168
Ben Hecht	117
Don Herold	33
James Wong Howe	156
Louis L'Amour	87, 93, 165
Gene Lockhart	92, 101
Ernst Lubitsch	6
Tom Mix	14
José Rodriguez	105
Sigmund Romberg	9
William Saroyan	41, 44, 51, 56, 58, 67
Dore Schary	73
Upton Sinclair	16
Herb Sterne	130, 137, 140, 148, 152
Dalton Trumbo	161
Jim Tully	20, 30
Rob Wagner	1, 46
Irving Wallace	76
Jessamyn West	116